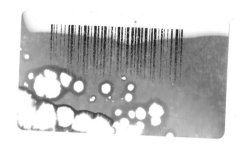

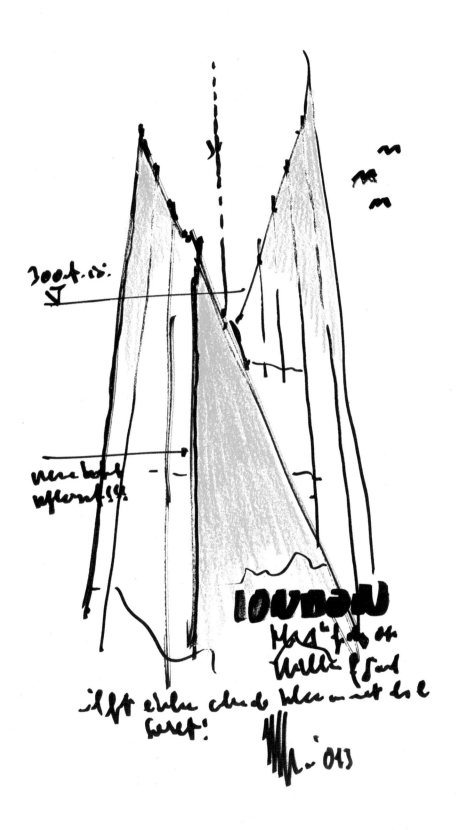

LONDON

wrist.

southwark.
the critinium
of southern

LONDON
THE
SHARD.

LONDON BRIDGE TOWER

'03

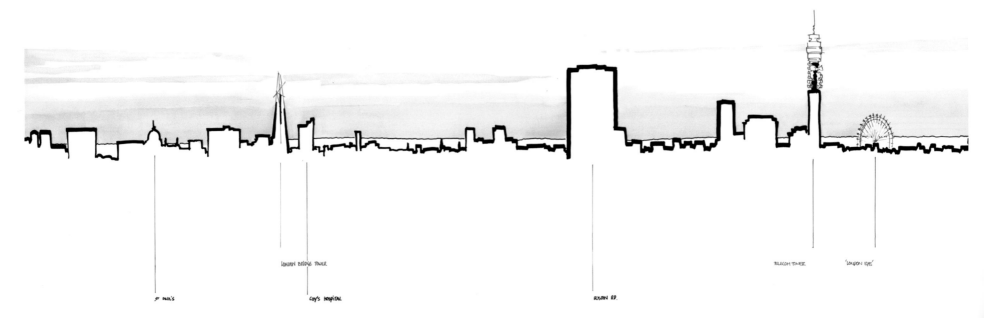

ST PAUL'S

LONDON BRIDGE TOWER

GUY'S HOSPITAL

EUSTON RD.

TELECOM TOWER

'LONDON EYE'

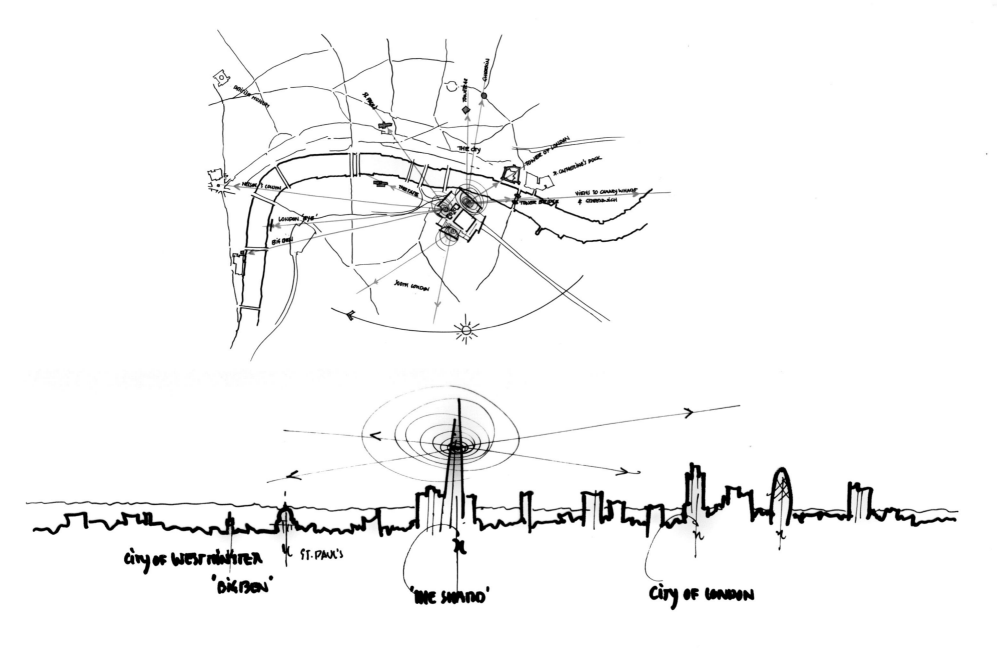

CITY OF WESTMINSTER

'BIG BEN'   ST. PAUL'S

'THE SHARD'   CITY OF LONDON

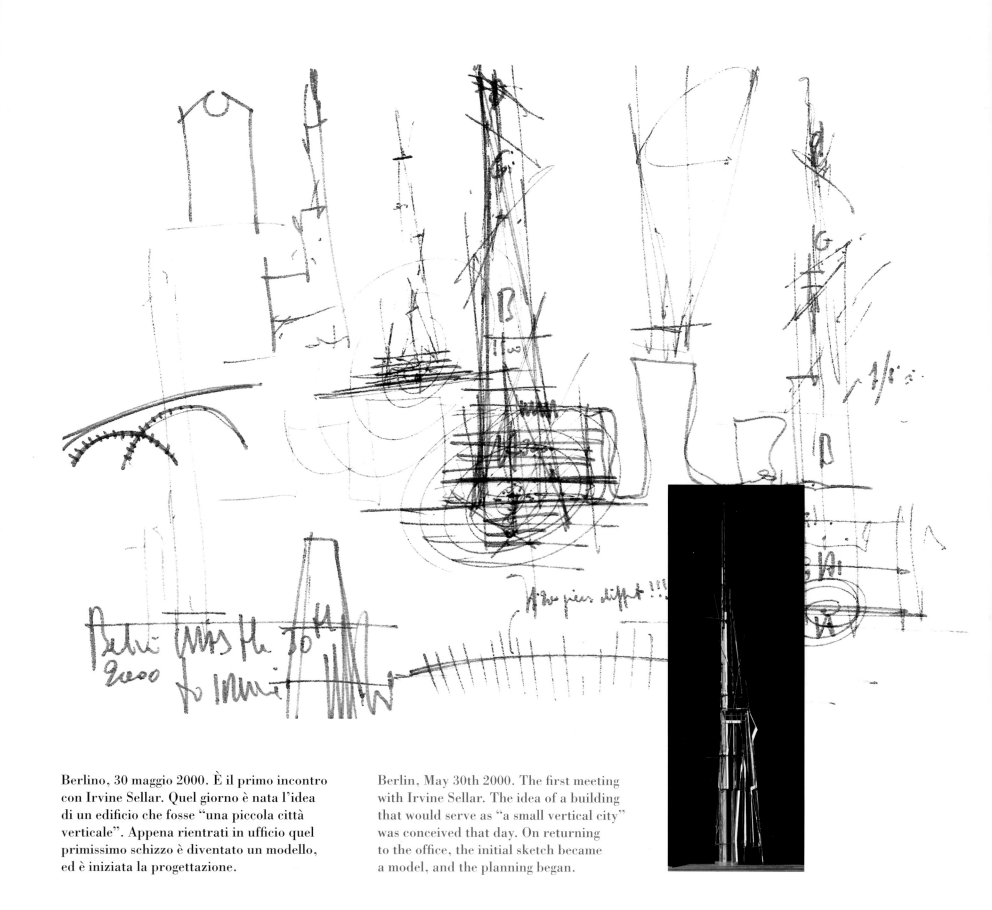

Berlino, 30 maggio 2000. È il primo incontro con Irvine Sellar. Quel giorno è nata l'idea di un edificio che fosse "una piccola città verticale". Appena rientrati in ufficio quel primissimo schizzo è diventato un modello, ed è iniziata la progettazione.

Berlin, May 30th 2000. The first meeting with Irvine Sellar. The idea of a building that would serve as "a small vertical city" was conceived that day. On returning to the office, the initial sketch became a model, and the planning began.

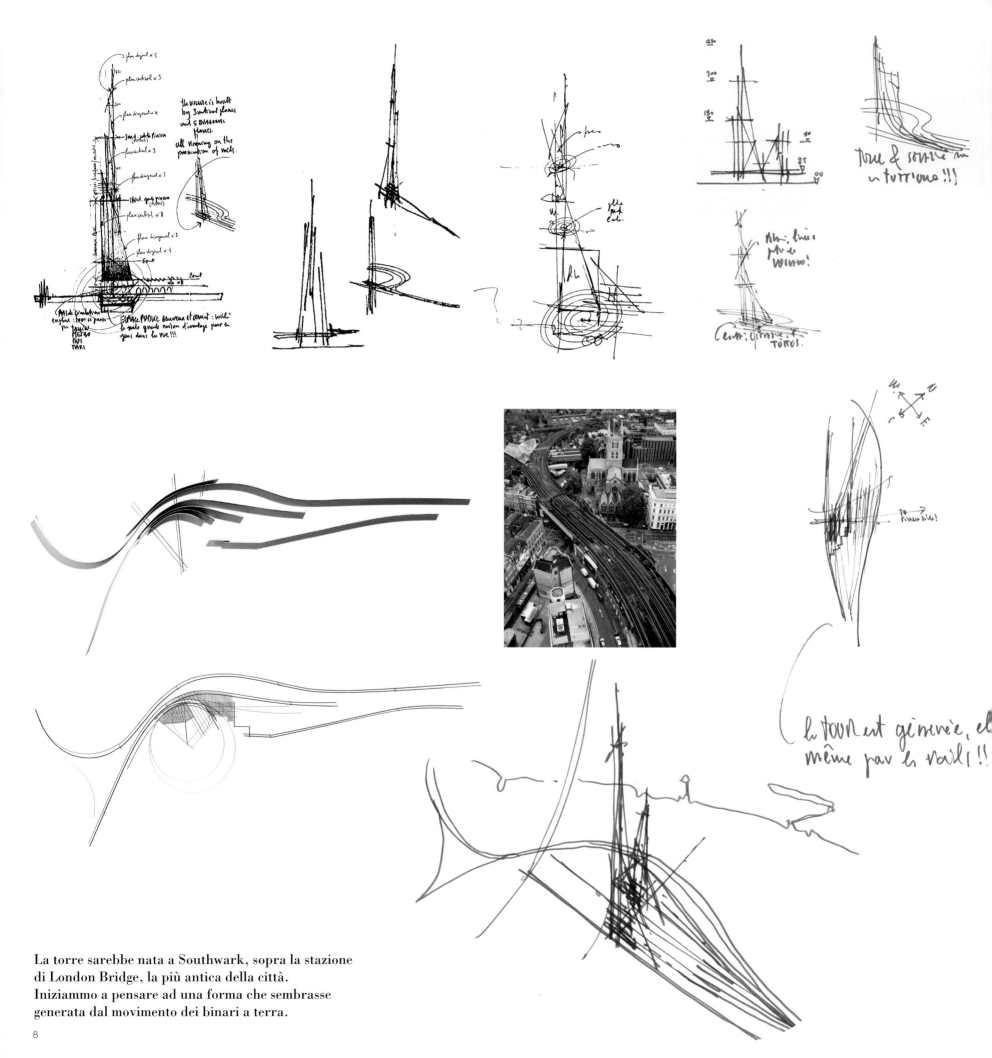

La torre sarebbe nata a Southwark, sopra la stazione
di London Bridge, la più antica della città.
Iniziammo a pensare ad una forma che sembrasse
generata dal movimento dei binari a terra.

8

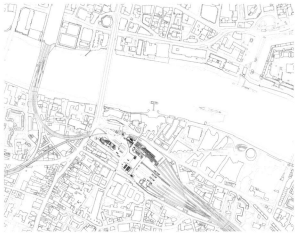

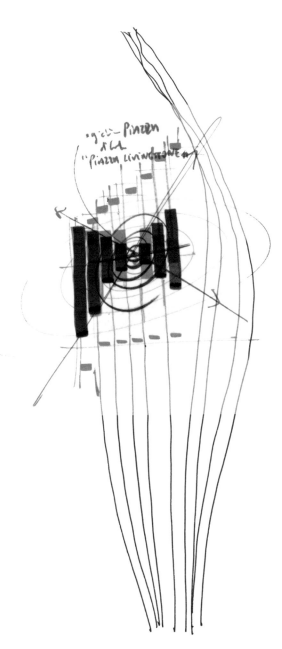

The tower would be built in Southwark, over
London Bridge Station, the oldest in the city. We began
to think of a shape that appeared as if it were generated
by the movement of the tracks on the ground.

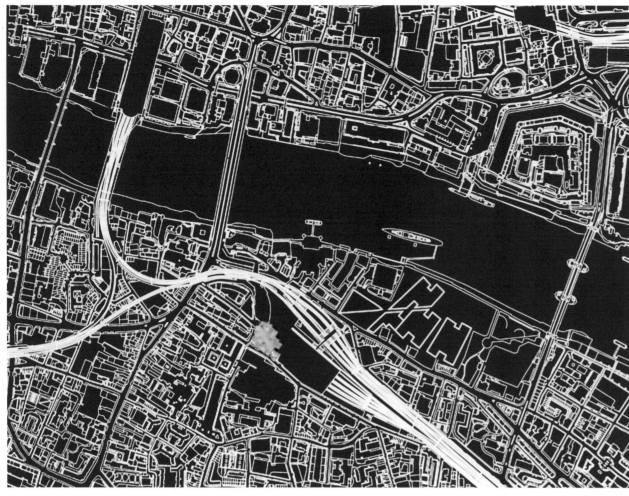

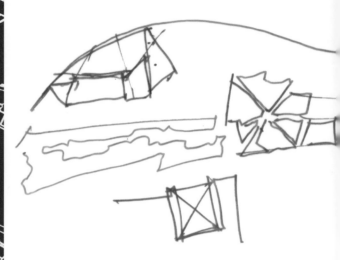

OPTION C

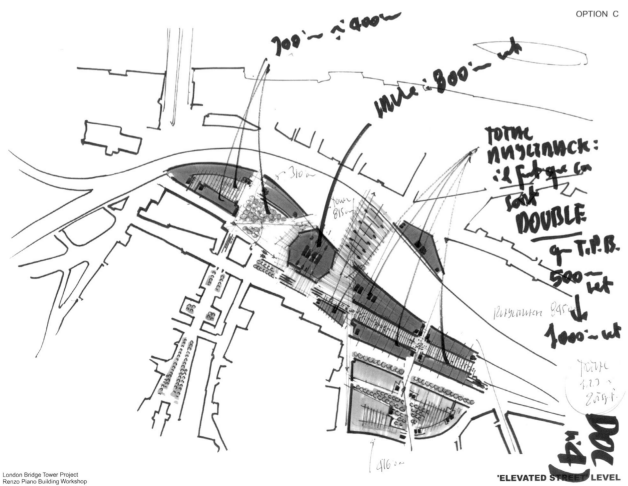

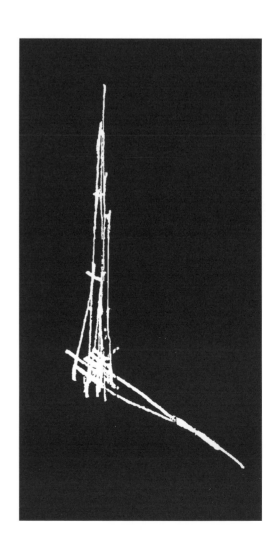

London Bridge Tower Project
Renzo Piano Building Workshop

July 2001

'ELEVATED STREET' LEVEL

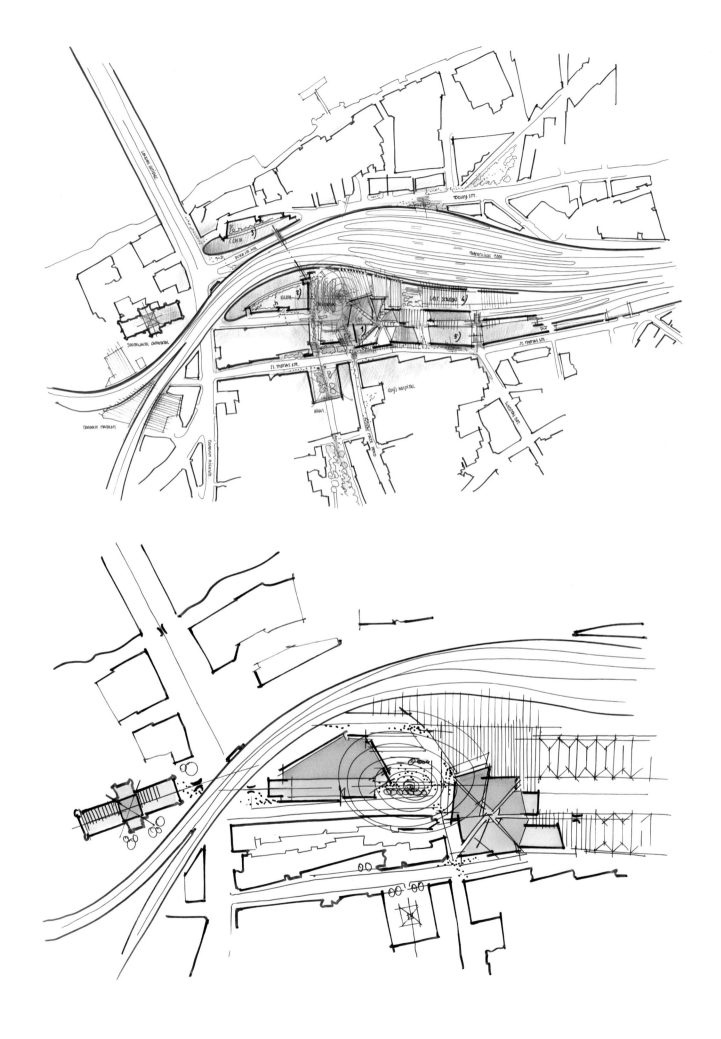

Per quanto possa sembrare sorprendente, la nascita del nome 'Shard' (scheggia) risale proprio al primo design workshop nel nostro ufficio di Genova, a settembre del 2000. Avevamo preparato un piccolo plastico, una semplice scheggia di legno che si integrava bene nel nostro micro-modello dell'area circostante, tra il fiume Tamigi e i binari ferroviari. Solo poche settimane prima avevamo visitato il sito insieme a Irvine Sellar, e la vista dalla cima delle Southwark Towers era stata rivelatrice per Renzo e il team: un fiume di acqua (il Tamigi) e un fiume di acciaio (i binari) scorrevano ai nostri piedi. Qualche mese prima avevamo lavorato al concorso di idee "Living In The City, an urban renaissance" per la realizzazione di progetti a Londra: in realtà era molto inusuale per RPBW partecipare a un concorso, ma Renzo pensava che sarebbe stato un utile esercizio creativo. Ripensandoci, credo che questo ci abbia davvero aiutato nel progettare lo Shard. È significativo il fatto che il Sindaco di Londra, Ken Livingstone, visitando l'esposizione, fosse entusiasta di fronte al potenziale di sviluppo che Londra dimostrava di avere: da allora è stato il maggiore sostenitore del nostro progetto.
Secondo me l'idea di Renzo di proporre, fin dall'inizio, un edificio a uso misto è stata un colpo di genio. E anche il fatto che Irvine lo abbia riconosciuto è stato altrettanto importante, ed è una prova di quell'acume e di quell'istinto che gli permettono di capire immediatamente cosa può funzionare. È importante ricordare che, all'epoca, a Londra il settore immobiliare considerava una torre a uso misto (commerciale, residenziale, ecc.) un affare di impossibile gestione, perché gli affitti decorrono in periodi diversi e sono quindi difficili da combinare. Irvine Sellar tuttavia lo vedeva come un modo per ridurre i rischi, e gli anni successivi, caratterizzati da una complessa situazione

economica, insieme al cambiamento nel valore da immobile uso ufficio a uso residenziale, hanno probabilmente provato quanto avesse ragione. Una volta accettata l'idea di una torre a uso misto, è stato possibile rendere l'edificio più slanciato verso l'alto, "per scomparire nel cielo".
Durante lo stesso periodo, RPBW lavorava al concorso per il New York Times Building, che avrebbe poi vinto.
Come tutti sappiamo, però, New York è caratterizzata da un contesto urbano completamente diverso rispetto a quello londinese: è una città verticale, con tante torri che si innalzano verso il cielo come una fitta foresta, mentre Londra è densa, addirittura caotica, e prevalentemente caratterizzata da altezze medio-basse, in particolare nella zona a sud del fiume. Evidentemente, progettare un edificio molto alto a Londra richiedeva un approccio totalmente diverso. L'area che Sellar aveva acquistato per la realizzazione del progetto era complessa: piccola e di forma irregolare, si estendeva in parte sopra la Stazione di London Bridge e in parte su St. Thomas Street, che è immediatamente adiacente a sud. St. Thomas Street è una delle strade più antiche di Londra, la via di accesso al London Bridge, che per lungo tempo è stato l'unico ponte per attraversare il fiume. Lo spazio edificabile era ricavato dalla spianata provocata da una bomba tedesca, durante la Seconda Guerra Mondiale, che aveva distrutto parte della stazione ferroviaria e aveva creato l'area per la costruzione, all'inizio degli anni settanta, delle Southwark Towers.
.....
Joost Moolhuijzen

As surprising as it may seem, the name Shard or the reference to a 'shard' occurred as early as the first design workshop at our Genoa office in September 2000. We had actually made a small model that was a simple piece or shard of wood that fitted nicely into our micro-model of the surrounding site, with the river Thames and the rail tracks. Some weeks earlier we had visited the site with Irvine Sellar. The views from the top of Southwark Towers were very revealing for Renzo and the team. A river of water (the Thames) and a river of steel (the railway tracks) were at our feet. A few months beforehand we had worked on an ideas competition for building in London, 'Living In The City, an urban renaissance'. It was very unusual for RPBW to participate in an ideas competition but Renzo felt it would be good to free up our ideas. In retrospect I think this really helped us with the design of the Shard. Significantly, the Mayor of London, Ken Livingstone, had visited the exhibition and was very excited about the potential for future development in London. He became our most important ally for the project. In my view, Renzo's idea to propose a mixed-use building on the site from day one was a masterstroke. The fact that Irvine recognized this was equally important and proof of his astute instinct to know what could work. It is important to remember that at the time the London commercial property sector considered that a mixed-use tower with different uses (commercial, residential etc) stacked on top of one other was bad business sense and impossible to manage as the leases run over different periods and are difficult to combine. Irvine Sellar however saw it as reducing risk; the subsequent tumultuous economic years and shift of value from office to residential property has probably proven Irvine right.

Of course once the idea of a mixed-use tower had been accepted this allowed us to make the building more slender towards the top, 'to disappear into the sky'. During this period RPBW simultaneously worked on the competition for the New York Times Building, which we won. New York has a completely different urban context to London as we all know. In New York you have an extrusion of vertical towers like trees in a dense forest. London is completely different, dense even chaotic at times and largely mid to low rise, especially south of the river. Evidently designing a very tall building for London demanded a completely different approach. The site Sellar had acquired for the project is complex. Small, with an irregular shape, it perches partly on top of London Bridge Station and partly on St. Thomas Street, immediately adjacent to the south. St. Thomas Street is one of the oldest streets in London and used to function as the gateway to London Bridge, for a long time the only bridge crossing the river. The fact that a site for a building existed there at all was because a German bomb had destroyed part of the train station during the Second World War, creating space for the construction of an unsightly tower in the early seventies, Southwark Towers.
.....

Joost Moolhuijzen

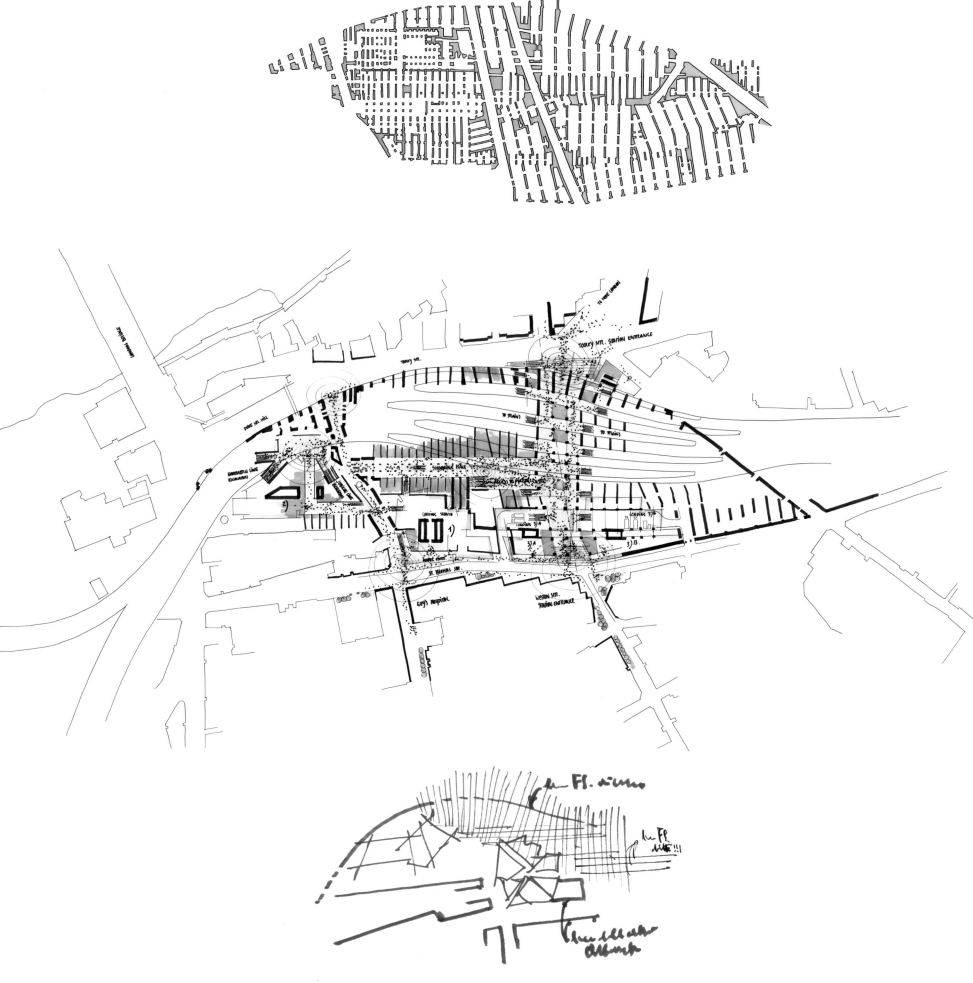

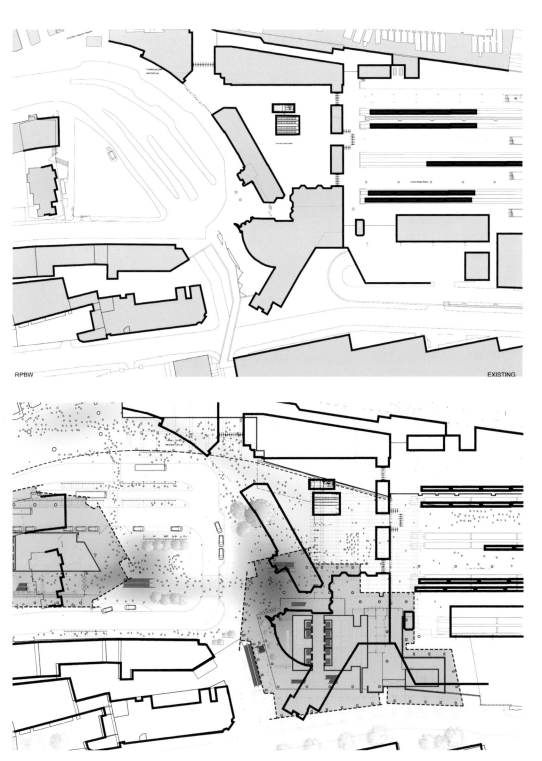

RPBW

EXISTING

Il quartiere prima dell'intervento.
Per realizzare il progetto sono stati demoliti due edifici:
Southwark Towers e New London Bridge House.

The existing site. Two buildings were demolished
in order to build the project: Southwark Towers
and New London Bridge House.

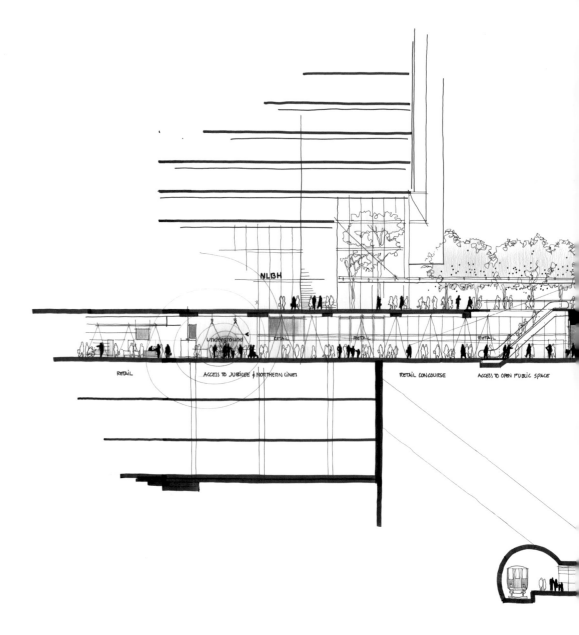

.....

Fino dal primo giorno ci aspettava un'altra sfida: il Public Realm. Infatti non è possibile immaginare di costruire una torre nel bel mezzo di Londra senza preoccuparsi dell'impatto sul sito intorno ad essa.

Non riesco a pensare a un'altra torre che tocchi il terreno in maniera tanto leggera come lo Shard: abbiamo tolto volume ai livelli inferiori dell'edificio per restituirlo nello spazio aperto pubblico, riadattando il 35% dell'area a livello della hall e il 15% a livello di St. Thomas Street. Eppure, l'edificio continuava a evidenziare un indice di sfruttamento di 32 a 1, un valore elevato perfino secondo gli standard di Hong Kong o New York!

Fortunatamente non sapevamo ancora che sfida formidabile avremmo dovuto affrontare per migliorare il Public Realm intorno, in particolare per quanto concerne la stazione ferroviaria: per noi il progetto non aveva senso se non comprendeva anche la copertura e l'atrio del nodo ferroviario esistente. Infatti solo i viaggiatori allenati da anni di pendolarismo riuscivano a orientarsi in quell'ambiente disagevole e disorientante. Dovevamo fare qualcosa. Naturalmente la nostra torre avrebbe beneficiato dal restyling della stazione, ma questa non è mai stata la nostra motivazione principale: appariva semplicemente come una grande opportunità per migliorare la zona circostante. Questo ampliamento del progetto è stato imposto per legge dall'accordo contenuto nella Sezione 106, che dispone l'obbligo di finanziamento a progetti pubblici locali da parte delle iniziative private di sviluppo urbano. In pratica, è un po' come progettare e finanziare i lavori di ristrutturazione nel cortile del vicino durante la costruzione della propria casa: il vostro vicino, probabilmente, si sarà fatto un'idea in merito a quello che proponete di costruire, e potrebbe essere riluttante e poco collaborativo nei vostri confronti. E questo è stato più o meno quello che è successo a noi, ma su una scala più grande. Non si dovrebbero sottovalutare le difficoltà legate alla ricostruzione di un nuovo atrio ferroviario dove transitano 300.000 passeggeri ogni giorno: se qualcosa va storto le implicazioni sono molto serie. Inevitabilmente, le procedure di autorizzazione che si applicano quando si lavora in questo tipo di ambiente sono molto severe e, sfortunatamente, non aiutano sempre a mandare avanti il progetto (a volte, addirittura, sono state usate come scuse per evitare di prendere delle decisioni).

Negli anni, abbiamo probabilmente speso più energie su questa parte del progetto che su qualunque altro aspetto necessario a farlo proseguire nella giusta direzione. Nel lavoro di un architetto è la parte invisibile dell'iceberg: il risultato finale è sotto gli occhi di tutti, ma la strada per giungervi può essere tortuosa. Londra è un luogo particolare in termini di pianificazione urbana.

È una città di mercanti dove quasi tutto è negoziabile; non sono stati fatti importanti piani urbanistici generali in passato e nemmeno ne esistono oggi, come invece accade in altre città come Parigi. La nostra sfida è stata trovare il giusto equilibrio tra quanto era auspicabile in questo contesto e quanto era effettivamente realizzabile. Insieme al Southwark Council abbiamo sviluppato un piano di inquadramento per l'area del London Bridge: non si tratta di un rigido piano urbanistico, bensì della definizione di una serie di proposte specifiche per quell'area. In questo contesto nel 2004 il cliente voleva acquisire la New London Bridge House, proprio di fronte alla stazione ferroviaria e alle Southwark Towers, l'area dove sarebbe sorto lo Shard. Lo sviluppo di questa parte del progetto ci ha permesso di migliorare ulteriormente l'area pubblica, ben oltre la stessa stazione, convincendo gli urbanisti che la stazione esistente degli autobus TFL (Transport For London), costituita da 15 pensiline e ubicata di fronte all'ingresso dello Shard, avrebbe dovuto essere spostata così da allinearsi verso nord con i binari ferroviari, e creare una linea di connessione visiva che dalla stazione arrivava fino al London Bridge. Così siamo riusciti a creare una piccola ma importante piazza tra lo Shard e la London Bridge Area (il nostro progetto sull'ex New London Bridge House). Qui, nel 2006, abbiamo potuto fare quello che nel 2003 era ancora solo un sogno lontano. Incidentalmente, è stato proprio in base a presunte insufficienti migliorie alla realtà esistente che il CABE (Commission for Architecture and the Built Environment) ha avanzato obiezioni al progetto all'epoca della Public Inquiry sullo Shard. Fortunatamente, l'idea di creare un piano di inquadramento per tutta l'area è stata accettata dall'Ispettore e messa in pratica del nostro team un paio di anni più tardi.

J.M.

.....

One other aspect was on the drawing board from day one: the Public Realm. You cannot construct a tall building in the middle of London if it does not have a profoundly positive impact on the immediate surroundings. I cannot think of any other tall building which touches the ground as lightly as the Shard. We have taken away volumes at the lower levels of the building and given them over to public open space: 35% of the site at concourse level is given over and 15% at St. Thomas street level. Even after doing this, the building still has a plot ratio of 32 to 1, which is high even by Hong Kong or New York standards!

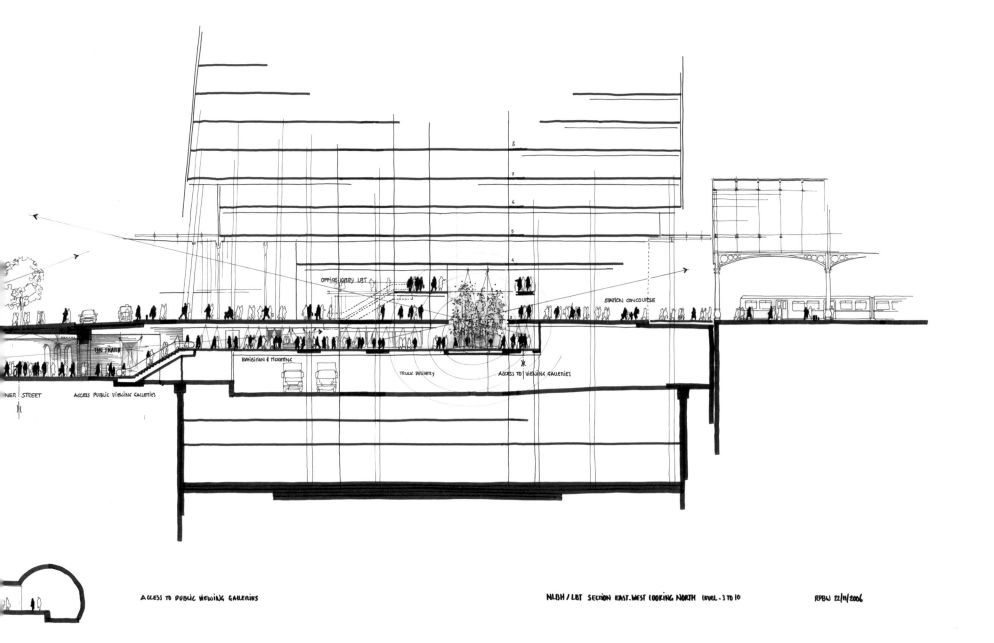

ACCESS TO PUBLIC VIEWING GALLERIES   NLBH / LBT SECTION EAST-WEST LOOKING NORTH LEVEL -3 TO 10   RPBW 22/11/2006

It is fortunate that we did not know in advance how formidable the challenge would be to improve the public realm, especially in relation to the adjacent train station. For us it has always been an integral part of the project to make improvements to the existing station nodus roof and concourse. Only battle-hardened commuters would find their way in this unfriendly and disorienting environment. Something had to be done. Of course our tower would benefit from a refit of the station but this was never our main motivation: it simply seemed like a great opportunity to improve this area. In legal terms this was enforced by what is called a Section106 Agreement, where private development is obliged to fund local public projects. The tricky part of this agreement is that it is a bit like designing and paying for improvements to your neighbour's yard, while building your own house next door. Your neighbour is likely to have an opinion about what you propose, and potentially be reluctant, even uncooperative. This is more or less what happened, on a grander scale. One should not underestimate the difficulty of rebuilding a new station concourse through which 300,000 passengers pass daily. If anything goes

wrong the implications are very serious. Inevitably there are extensive approval procedures to be followed when working in this kind of environment. Unfortunately these procedures were not always helpful in moving the project forward (and were sometimes used as excuses to avoid making decisions). Over the years we probably spent more energy on this part of the project than anything else to keep it moving in the right direction. This is the invisible part of the iceberg of an architect's work. We see the end result but the road to get there can be tortuous at times. London is a peculiar place when it comes to urban planning, interesting but still peculiar. It is a city of merchants where almost everything is negotiable; no grand masterplans have been executed or exist as they do in cities like Paris. Our challenge has been to navigate between what is desirable in this context and what is deliverable. With Southwark Council we developed a Framework Plan for the London Bridge area. It is not a fixed masterplan, but it established a framework of proposals for the area. In this context the client had the vision to acquire New London Bridge House in 2004 just opposite the train station and Southwark towers, the site

of the Shard. The development of this side of the site allowed us to fulfil the framework thinking and improve the public realm further, beyond the Station itself. We convinced the planners that the existing TFL (Transport For London) bus station of 15 bus stands, located in front of the entrance to the Shard, should rotate to align with the train tracks and move to the North to create clear sight lines from the train station through London Bridge. With this move we were able to create a small but important piazza between The Shard and London Bridge Place (our project on the site of the former New London Bridge House). Here we would be able to deliver in 2006 what we could only wish for in 2003. Incidentally it was on the subject of supposed insufficient improvements to the public realm that CABE (the Commission for Architecture and the Built Environment) objected to the project at the time of the Shard's Public Inquiry. Fortunately the idea of creating a framework plan for the site was welcomed by the Inquiry inspector and acted upon by our team a couple of years later.
J.M.
.....

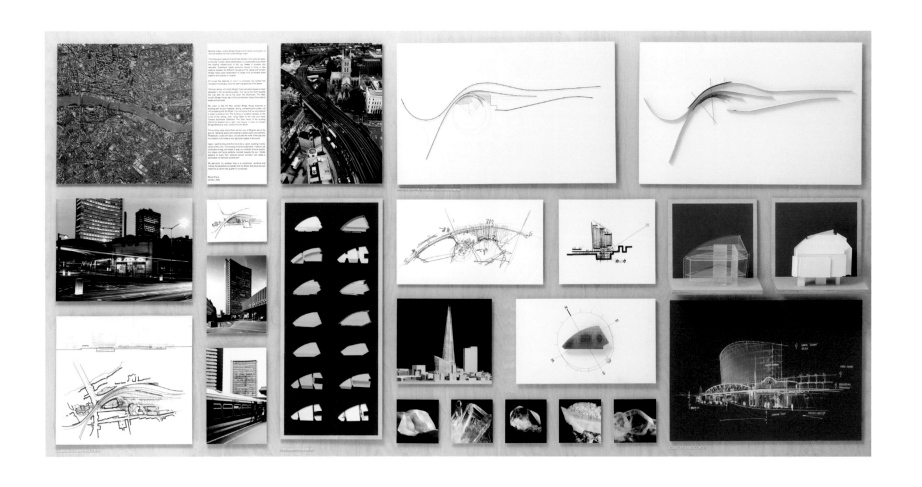

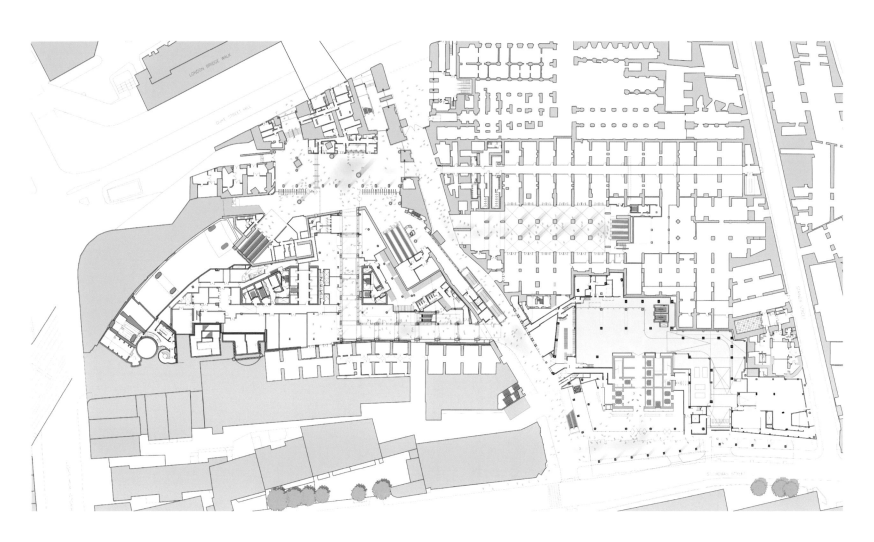

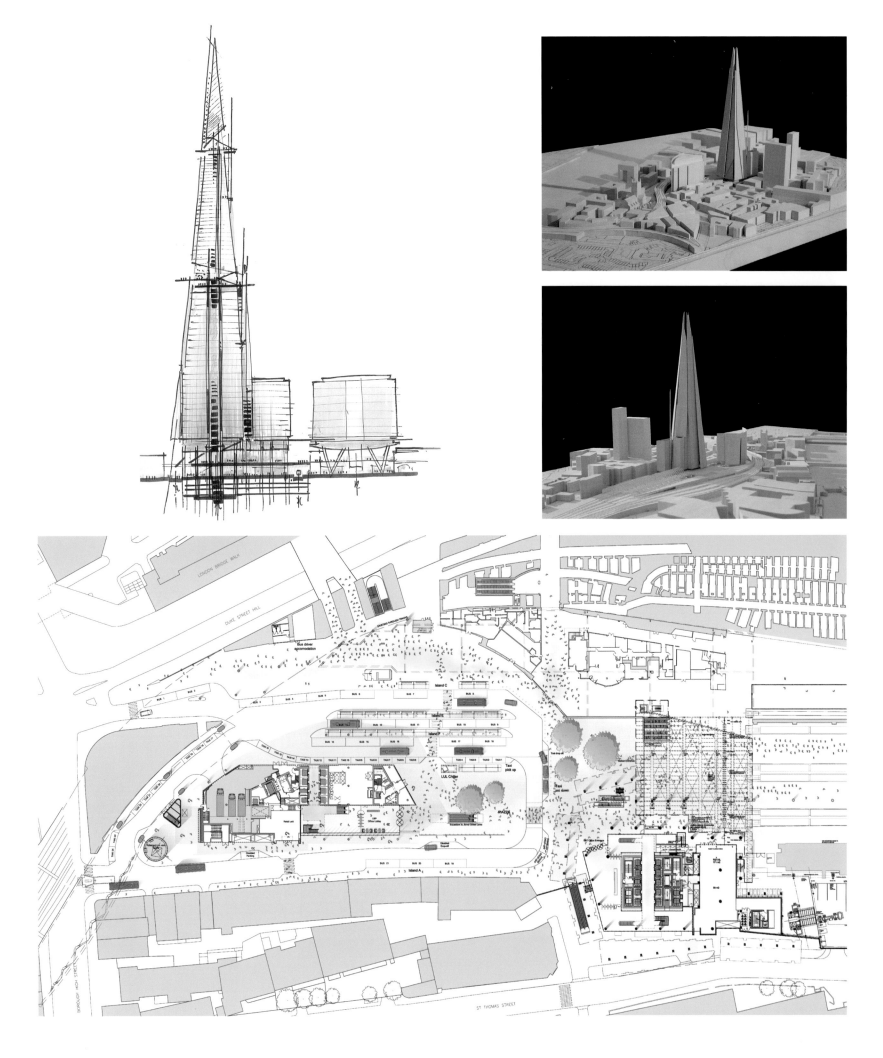

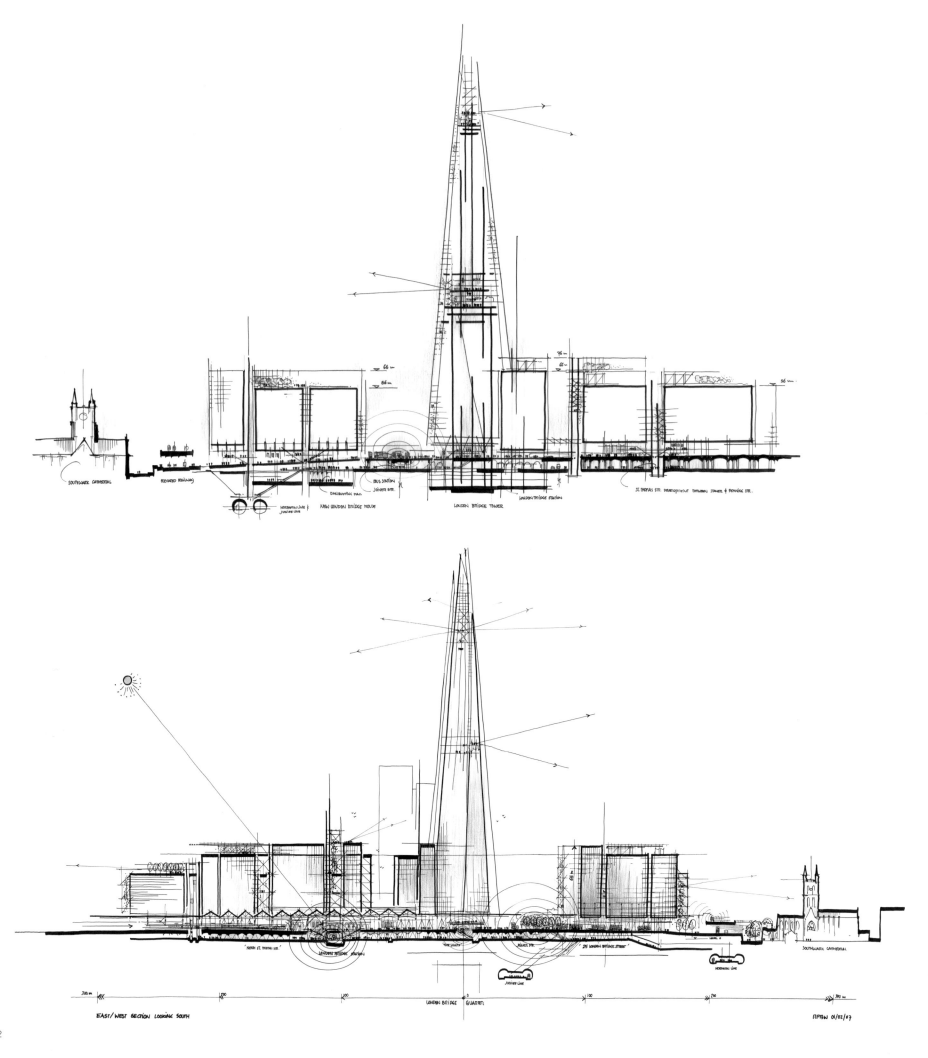

SOUTHWARK CATHEDRAL   BERMARD RAILWAY   NORTHERN LINE & JUBILEE LINE   BANQUETING HALL   BUS STATION JOINER STR.   NEW LONDON BRIDGE HOUSE   LONDON BRIDGE TOWER   LONDON BRIDGE STATION   ST. THOMAS STR. DEVELOPMENT BETWEEN JOINER & FENNING STR.

NORTH ST. THOMAS STR.   LONDON BRIDGE STATION   "THE SHARD"   JOINER STR.   25 LONDON BRIDGE STREET   JUBILEE LINE   NORTHERN LINE   SOUTHWARK CATHEDRAL   LONDON BRIDGE QUARTER

300 m   200   100   0   100   200   300 m

EAST/WEST SECTION LOOKING SOUTH   RPBW 01/02/07

22

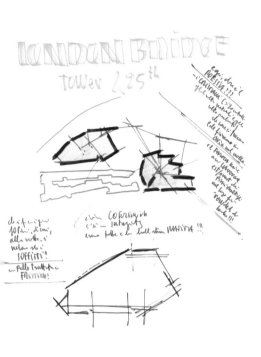

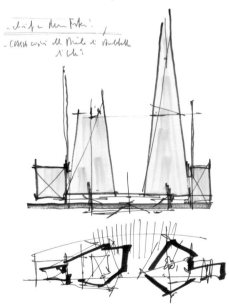

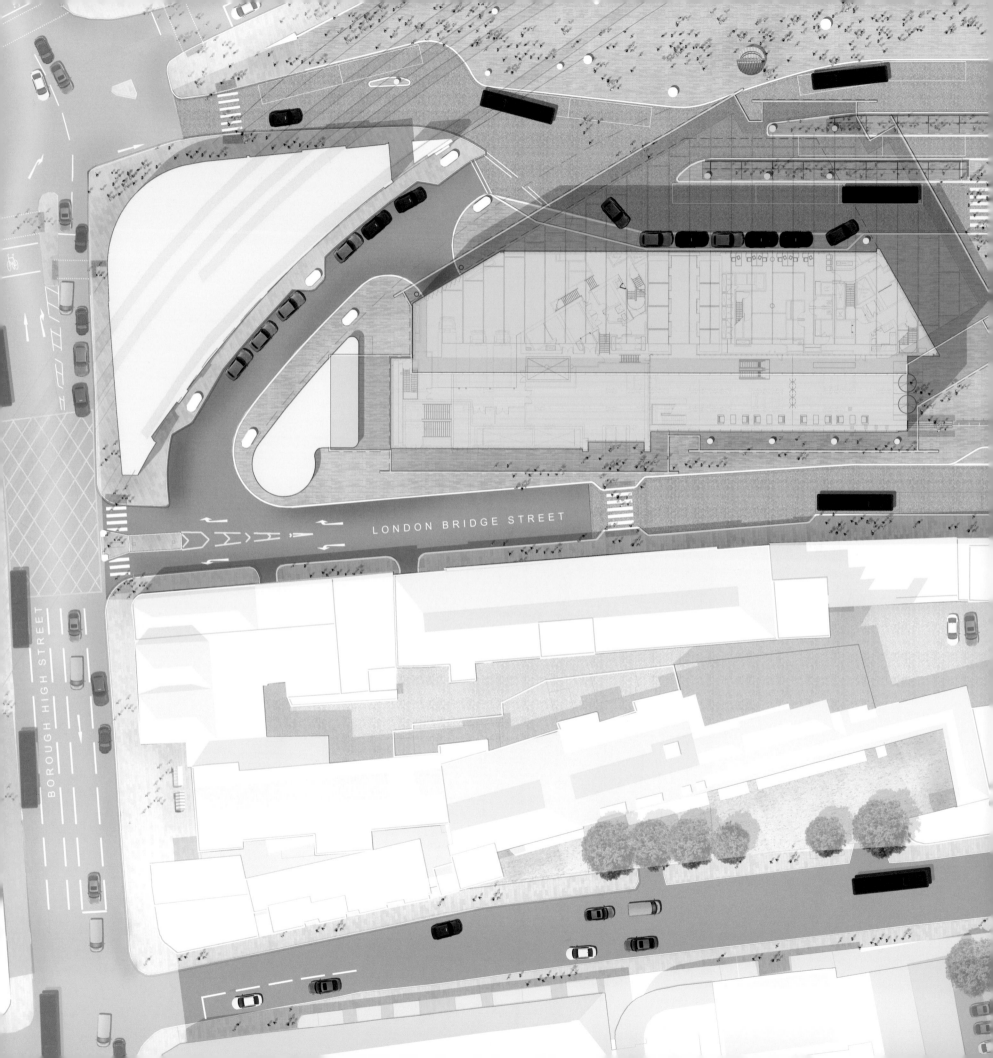

LONDON BRIDGE STREET

BOROUGH HIGH STREET

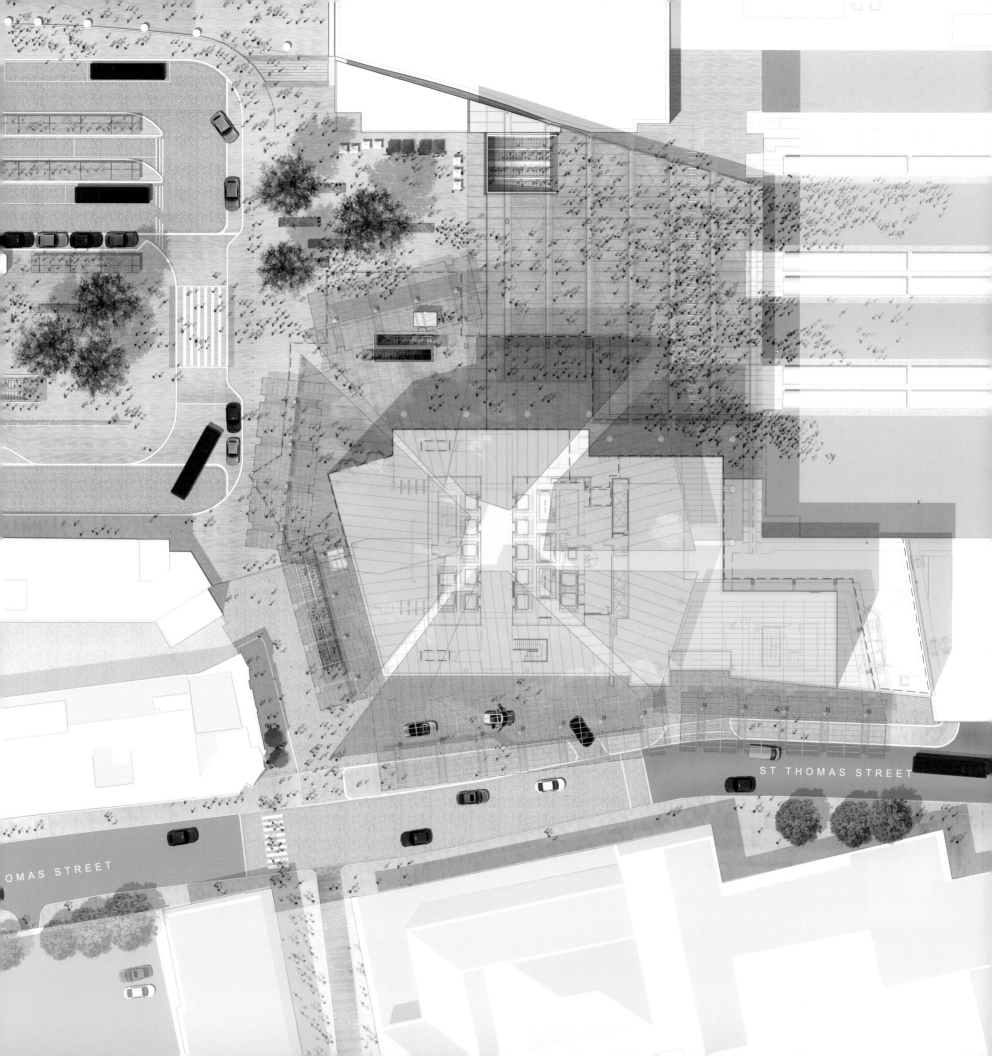

ST THOMAS STREET

OMAS STREET

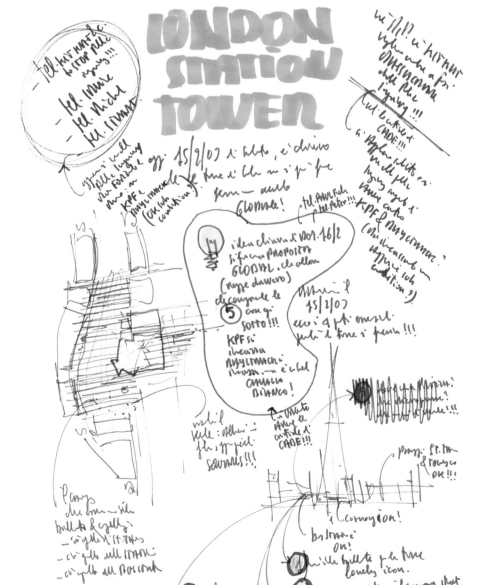

Miss A. Gerry
Decision Officer
Planning Central Casework Division
Office of the Deputy Prime Minister
Zone 3/J1, Eland House
Bressenden Place
London SW1E 5DU

Direct line: 020 7944 8708
Fax: 020 7944 5929
Web site: www.odpm.gov.uk

**OFFICE OF THE
DEPUTY PRIME MINISTER**

Berwin Leighton Paisner
Adelaide House,
London Bridge,
London EC4R 9HA

Our Ref: APP/A5840/V/02/1095887
Your Ref: TSTH.20855.1

18 November 2003

Dear Sirs

**TOWN AND COUNTRY PLANNING ACT 1990 – SECTION 77
LAND ADJOINING LONDON BRIDGE STATION, AT ST THOMAS STREET/JOINER
STREET, LONDON SE1.
APPLICATION BY TEIGHMORE LIMITED.
APPLICATION NO. 0100476**

1.   I am directed by the First Secretary of State to say that consideration has been given to the report of the Inspector, Mr John L Gray, DipArch MSc Registered Architect, who held a public local inquiry on 15-17, 22-25 and 28-30 April and 1,6,7 and 9 May 2003 into your client's application for planning permission (as amended) for the demolition of the existing Southwark Towers and construction of a mixed use building totalling 124,242sqm gross, comprising offices (Class B1), hotel (Class C1), fourteen apartments (Class C3), retail and restaurant uses (Class A1/A3), health and fitness club and associated servicing and car parking.

2.   The Secretary of State directed on 24 July 2002, in pursuance of section 77 of the Town and Country Planning Act 1990, that the application be referred to him instead of being dealt with by the local planning authority, the Council of the London Borough of Southwark.

3.   The Inspector, whose conclusions are reproduced in the annex to this letter, recommended that planning permission be granted subject to conditions. A copy of the Inspector's report is enclosed. All references to paragraph numbers, unless otherwise stated, are to that report. For the reasons given below the Secretary of State agrees with the Inspector's conclusions and recommendation that planning permission be granted.

4.   After the inquiry closed, the Secretary of State received letters from Berwin Leighton Paisner dated 25 July and Hepher Dixon dated 1 September. This correspondence has been taken into account by the Secretary of State in determining the application, but is not considered to raise any matters requiring wider reference back to the inquiry parties, either under Rule 17 of the Town and Country Planning (Inquiries Procedure) (England) Rules 2000, or in the interests of natural justice, prior to making his decision. Copies of this correspondence are not attached to this letter but can be made available upon written request to the above address. In addition, the Secretary of State has received a number of E Mails in support of the proposal.

La Public Inquiry per la richiesta di approvazione del progetto si è tenuta nel mese di aprile del 2003, ed è stata presieduta dall'Ispettore John Gray. I principali oppositori erano le commissioni English Heritage e Historic Royal Palaces, che temevano soprattutto un impatto sulla visibilità della cattedrale di St. Paul da Parliament Hill e Kenwood, nonché sullo sfondo su cui si staglia la Torre di Londra. L'Ispettore ha rifiutato entrambe le argomentazioni e l'Ufficio del Vice Primo Ministro, John Prescott, ha concesso l'approvazione condizionale il 18 novembre 2003.
.....
William Matthews

The Public Inquiry into the planning application took place in April 2003, chaired by the Inspector John Gray. The main opponents of the scheme were English Heritage and Historic Royal Palaces, and their principal concerns being the protected views of St. Paul's Cathedral from Parliament Hill and Kenwood, and the setting of the Tower of London.
The Inspector rejected both arguments and the Office of the Deputy Prime Minister, John Prescott, gave conditional approval on 18 November 2003.
.....
William Matthews

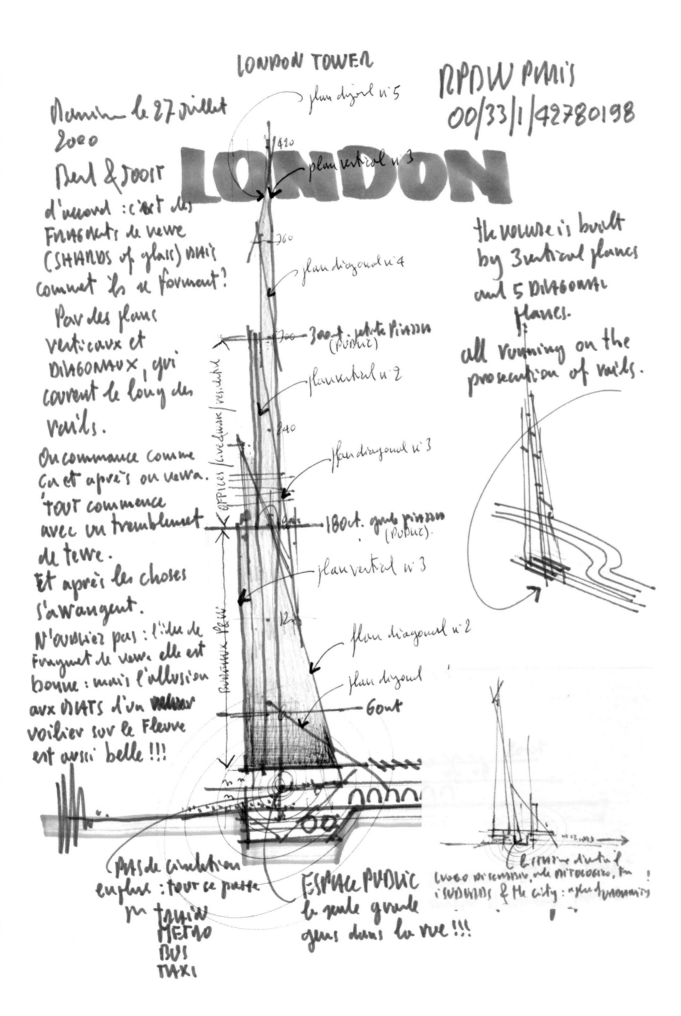

LONDON TOWER

RPBW PARIS
00/33/1/42780198

LONDON

the volume is built by 3 vertical planes and 5 DIAGONAL planes. all running on the prosecution of vails.

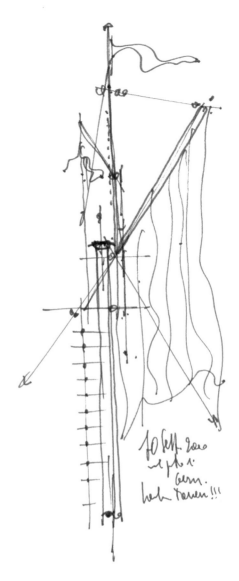

L'idea di salire in maniera sottile evocava un'immagine familiare di Londra. Pensavamo anche agli alberi delle navi che secoli fa attraccavano lungo il Tamigi.

The idea of rising subtly evoked a familiar image of London. We even referred to the masts of ships that docked centuries ago along the Thames.

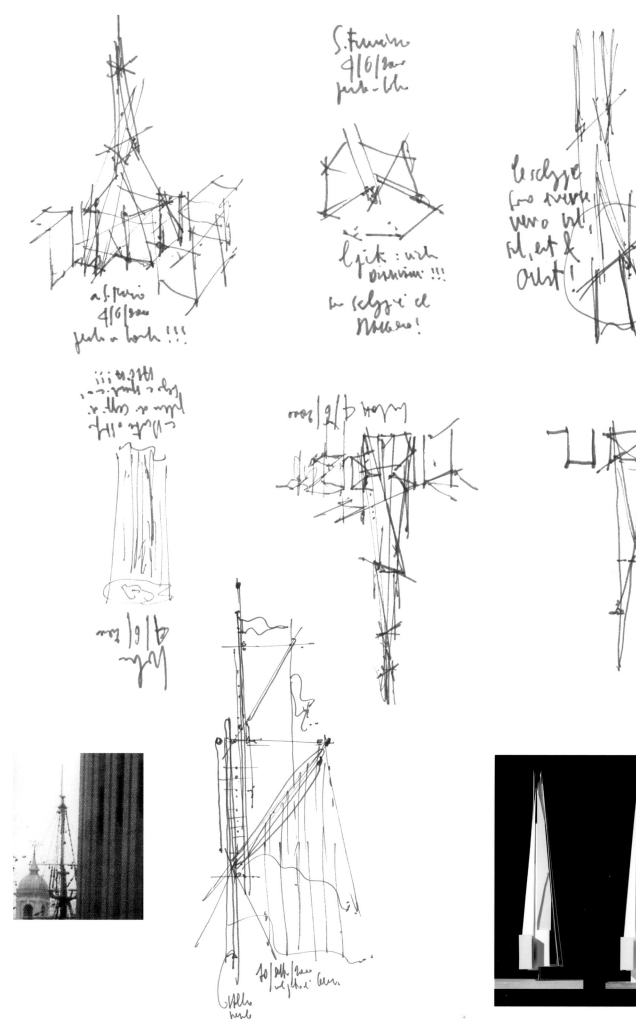

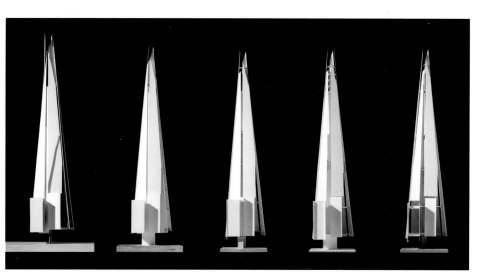

Late BRIDGE
June the 15th 2000

JOEST : lists made of
ABOUT 8 shards of glass.
We have to establish where each shard
starts and where it stops !!!

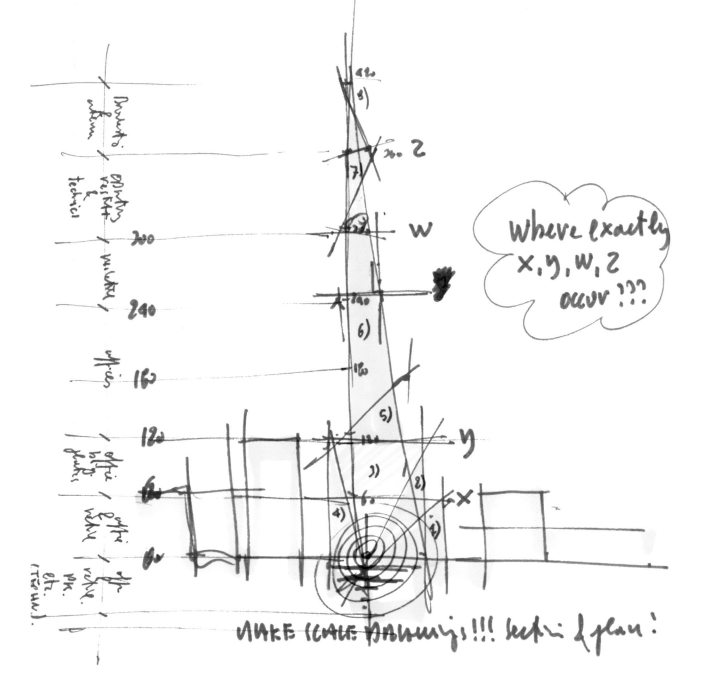

where exactly
x, y, w, z
occur ???

x. 2

w

y

x

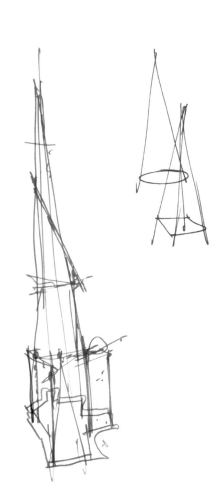

MAKE SCALE DRAWINGS!!!! section & plan!

34

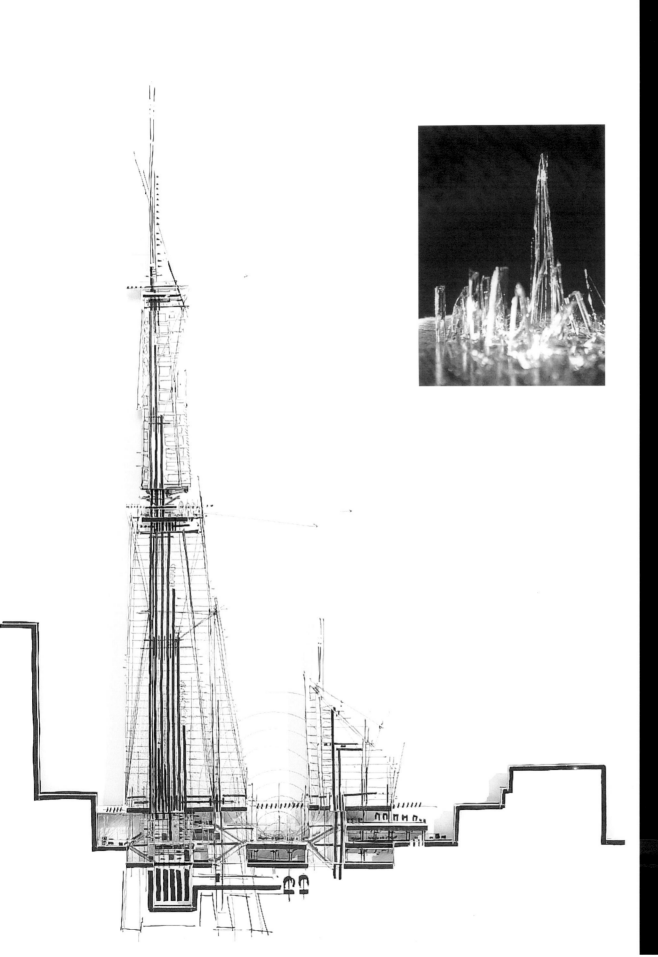

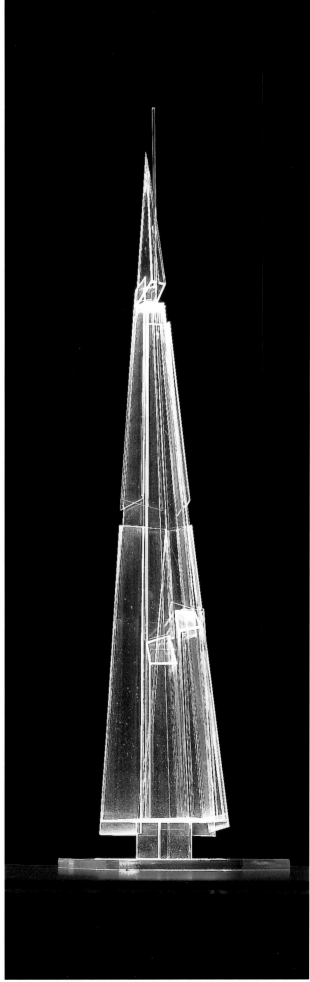

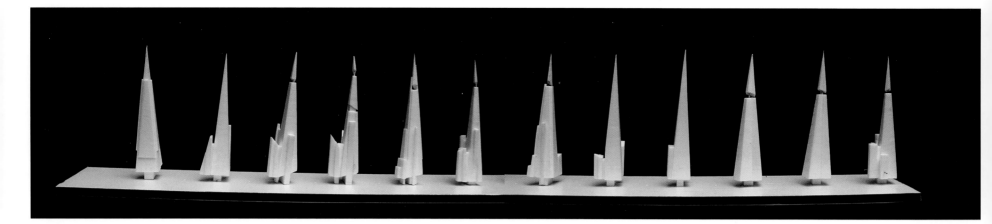

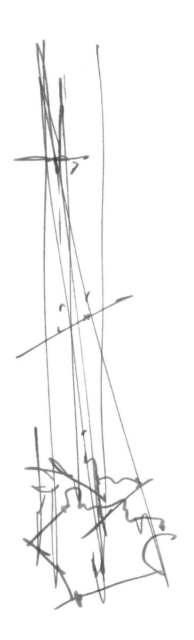  

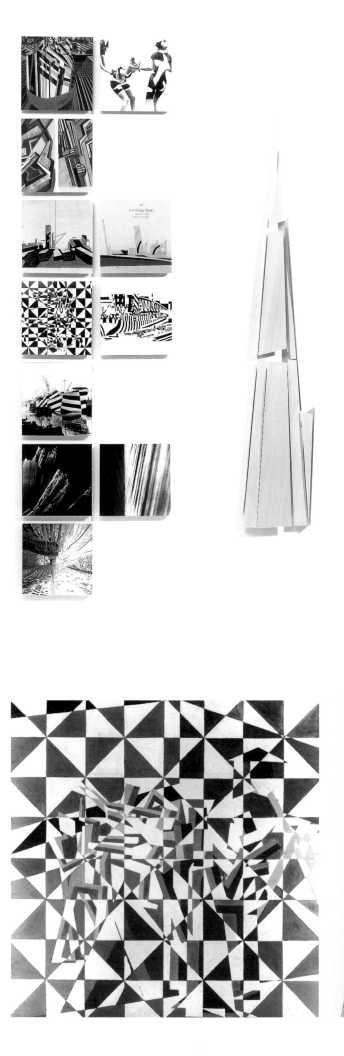

May 2000	First meeting with Irvine Sellar in Berlin at our Potsdamer Platz project
September 2000	First workshop in the Genoa office with Irvine Sellar & Barry Ostle Objective agreed to seek planning approval from Southwark Council before the end of the year for a 400 m high tower
October 2000	Switch from 400m to 300m high tower to comply with CAA (Civil Aviation Authority) height restriction of 1000 ft
March 2001	Planning application to Southwark Council
April 2003	Public Inquiry
November 2003	Planning approval granted by the Secretary of State
Jan 2004 – July 2005	Stage D design Shard
Sep 2005 – June 2006	Stage D Station & enabling works
June 2006 – April 2007	Stage E design Shard
June 2007 – Oct 2008	Stage F & G design Shard
November 2007	Mace appointed as main contractor to build the Shard
January 2008	Sellar sets up Qatari consortium for development of Shard & LBQ project
September 2008	Cancelled presentation to Qatari investors due to collapse of Lehmann brothers
Jan 2009 – Dec 2012	Stage H & L
February 2009	Demolition of Southwark towers completed
March 2009	Official start on site
July 2012	Shard physical completion
November 2012	Shard PC (practical completion)
February 2013	Opening of public viewing gallery
May 2013	Opening of Shangri La Hotel
April 2013	Opening of restaurants

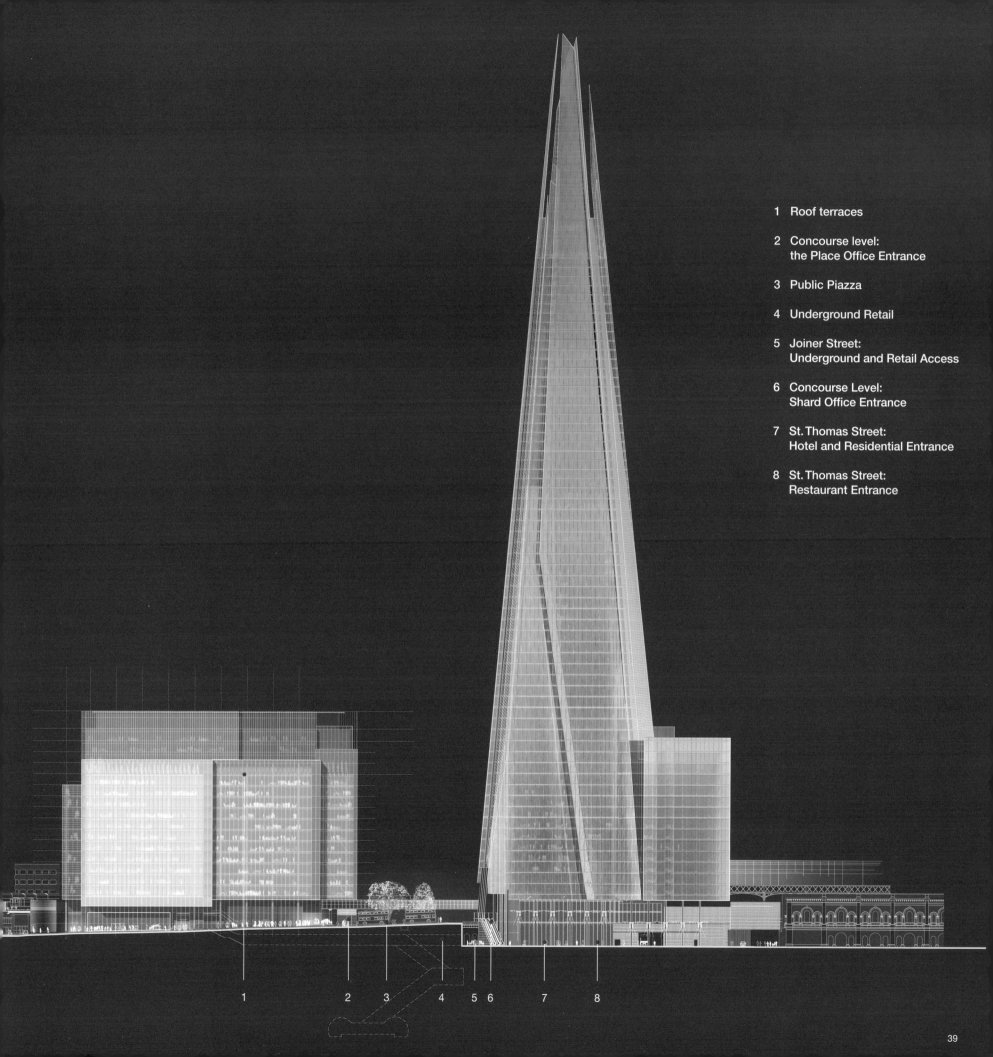

1 Roof terraces

2 Concourse level:
the Place Office Entrance

3 Public Piazza

4 Underground Retail

5 Joiner Street:
Underground and Retail Access

6 Concourse Level:
Shard Office Entrance

7 St. Thomas Street:
Hotel and Residential Entrance

8 St. Thomas Street:
Restaurant Entrance

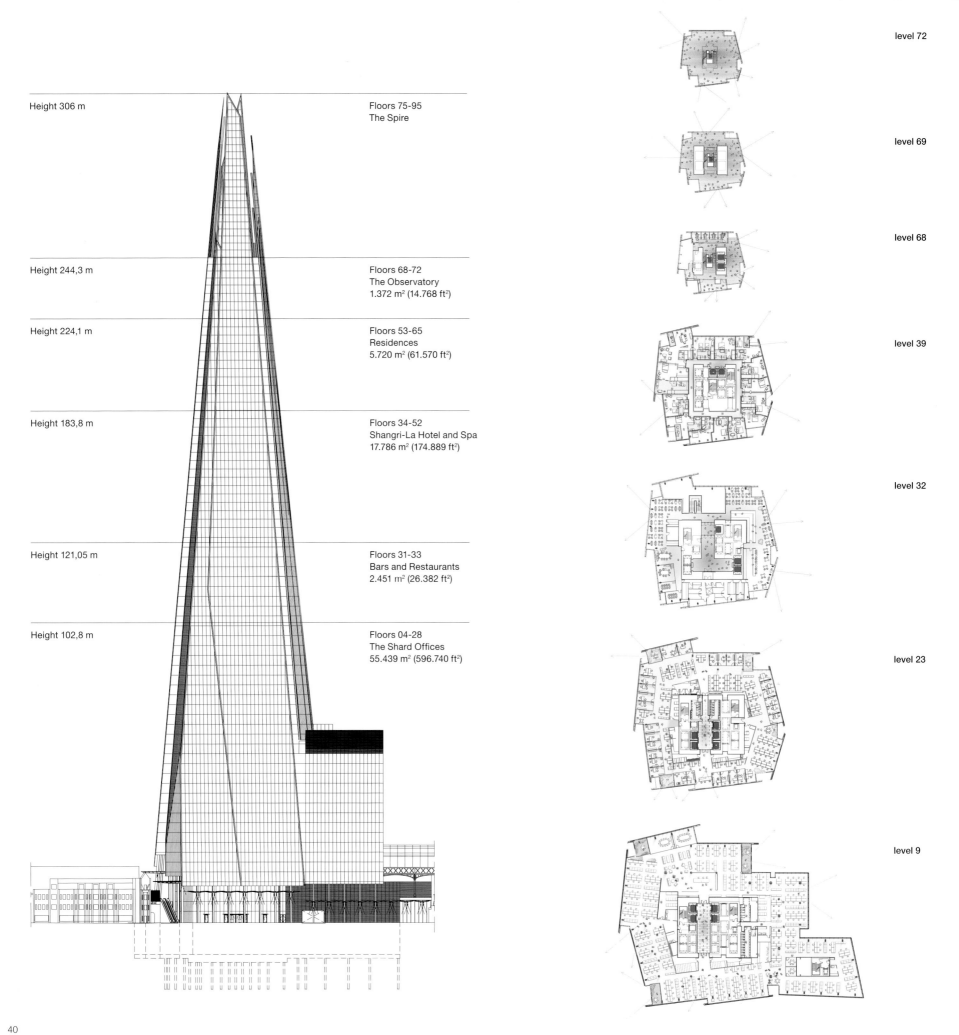

Height 306 m   Floors 75-95
The Spire

level 72

level 69

Height 244,3 m   Floors 68-72
The Observatory
1.372 m² (14.768 ft²)

level 68

Height 224,1 m   Floors 53-65
Residences
5.720 m² (61.570 ft²)

level 39

Height 183,8 m   Floors 34-52
Shangri-La Hotel and Spa
17.786 m² (174.889 ft²)

level 32

Height 121,05 m   Floors 31-33
Bars and Restaurants
2.451 m² (26.382 ft²)

level 23

Height 102,8 m   Floors 04-28
The Shard Offices
55.439 m² (596.740 ft²)

level 9

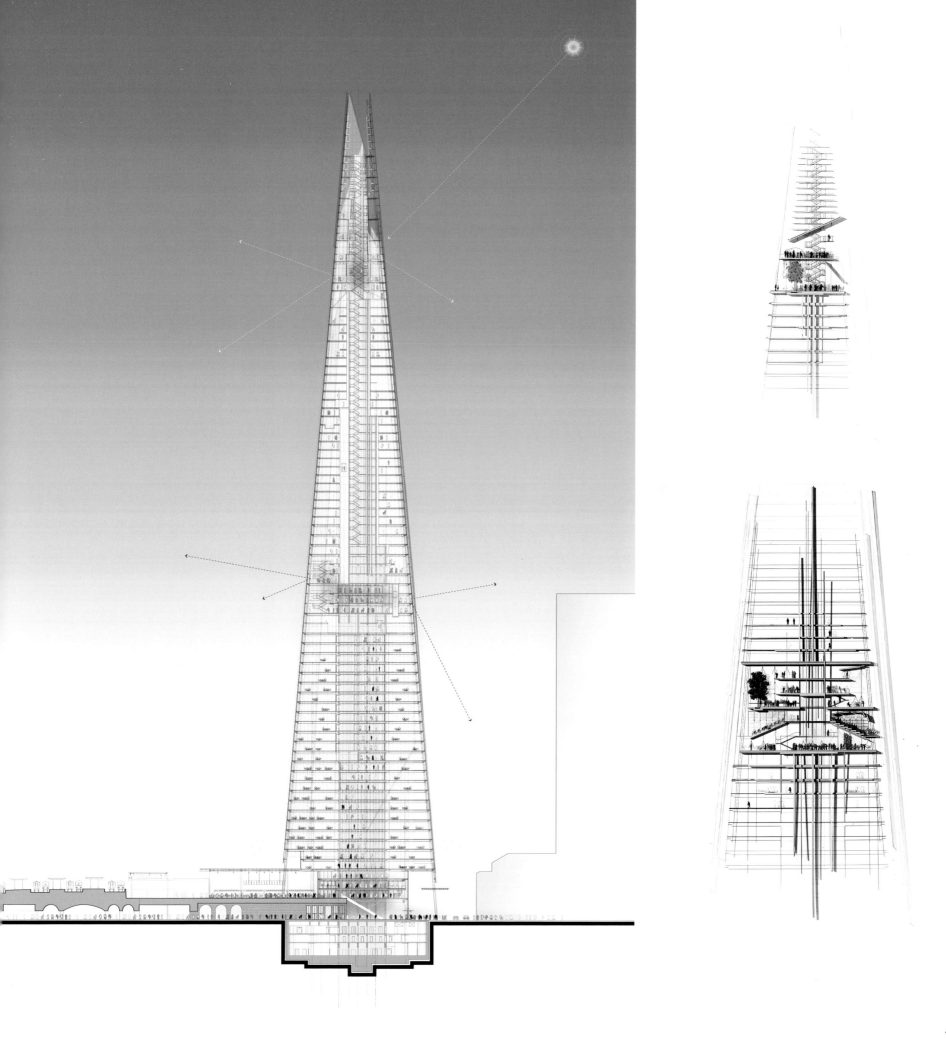

Come diceva Renzo, le torri possono avere una pessima reputazione e spesso la meritano: talvolta creano un ambiente sgradevole per i passanti a livello della strada, perché incanalano venti ad alta velocità, che possono creare raffiche lungo l'edificio o agli angoli. Già dalle primissime fasi di progettazione e come parte integrante del processo, abbiamo lavorato molto con RWDI in Canada per creare un ambiente ottimale per i pedoni. All'inizio la situazione era piuttosto scoraggiante: i primi risultati ottenuti nella galleria del vento suggerivano che avremmo dovuto coprire virtualmente l'intera St. Thomas Street con una pensilina che avrebbe mitigato il vento, ma che non avrebbe contribuito a creare un bell'ambiente urbano, e certamente avrebbe aumentato la concentrazione dei gas di scarico emessi dagli autobus londinesi. Tuttavia, con un po' di lavoro di cesello, una buona dose di testardaggine e innumerevoli prove e modelli siamo riusciti a giungere ad una soluzione più leggera, più permeabile e più urbana: la giustapposizione

e il gioco di diversi canopy in vetro a diverse altezze crea un luogo in scala umana rispetto al circondario, fatto di edifici e strade. L'altezza dei canopy è studiata in riferimento all'altezza dei tetti e del lungo muro arcato in mattoni del viadotto della stazione: ciò permette di integrare la torre nell'immediato vicinato, mentre la generosa ricaduta della facciata di ingresso dell'hotel a livello strada migliora ulteriormente il senso del luogo. Quando abbiamo iniziato a lavorare alla scelta della pavimentazione molti esperti, tra cui diversi agenti immobiliari, ci dicevano che eravamo matti. Ripensando ad allora, è un miracolo che Sellar sia rimasto dalla nostra parte, una banda di architetti stranieri, e non abbia permesso a opinioni esterne di influenzare in maniera sostanziale il progetto. Ora le pavimentazioni irregolari sono considerate un punto di forza dell'area, e creano ambienti di lavoro positivi e interessanti conferendo un senso di scala e di luogo.
J.M.
.....

As Renzo mentioned, towers can have a bad reputation and often they deserve it. They can create an unpleasant pedestrian environment at street level, in the way that they channel high wind speeds, and can force gusts down a building or around corners. From the early design stages and as part of the planning process we worked hard with RWDI in Canada to make sure we would create the right pedestrian environment.

At first it was somewhat discouraging. The first wind tunnel test results suggested we would need to cover virtually the whole of St. Thomas Street with canopies, which would be good for wind mitigation but not at all good for creating an urban environment let alone dealing with the exhaust fumes of the London buses.

But with fine-tuning, quite a bit of stubbornness and continuous re-modelling and re-testing, we arrived at a lighter, more permeable and more urban solution.

The juxtaposition, the play of the different glazed canopies at different heights creates a sense of place and a human scale in relation to the surrounding listed buildings and streetscape. The canopies form a datum level relating to the roof heights and top of the long arched brick wall of the station viaduct. They make the tower fit into its immediate surroundings; the generous setback of the street level facade of the Hotel entrance further enhances the sense of place. When we started working the typical floor plates many experts, including letting agents, told us we were mad. Looking back, it is a miracle that Sellar stood by us, a bunch of foreign architects, and did not let early third-party opinions influence the design substantially. Now the irregular floor plates are praised as an asset, creating good and interesting workplaces with a sense of scale and place.
J.M.
.....

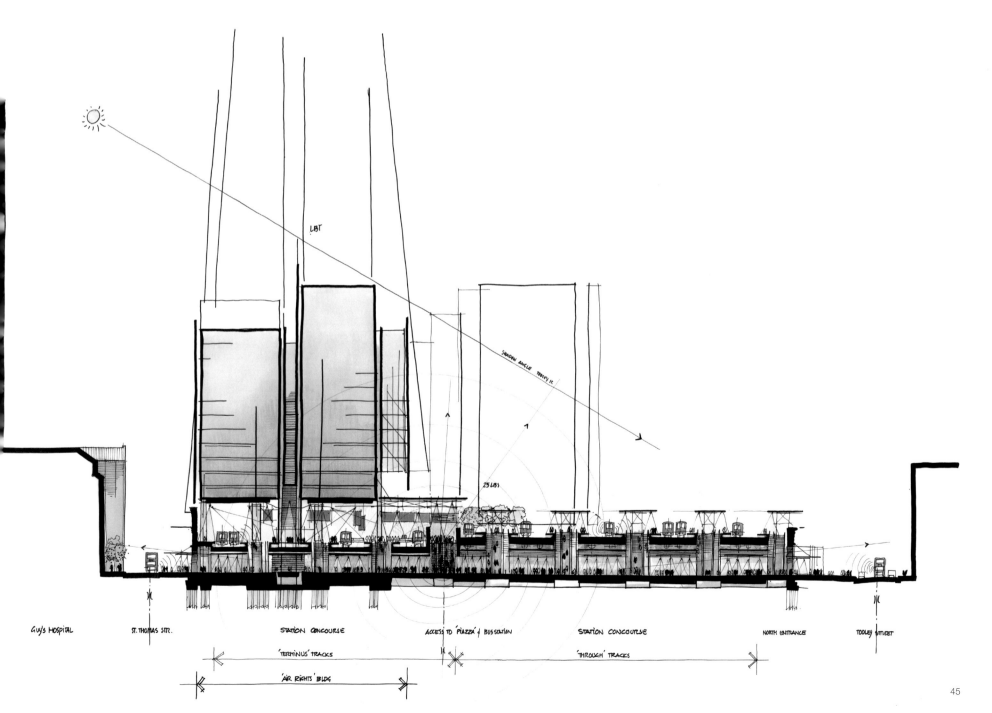

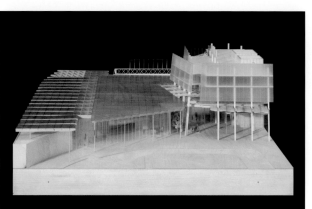

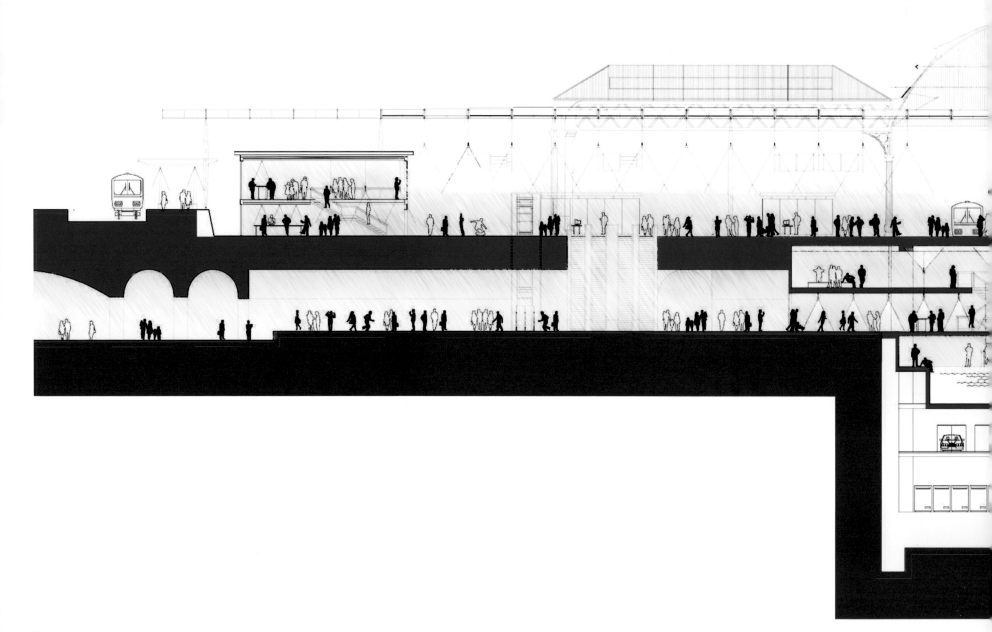

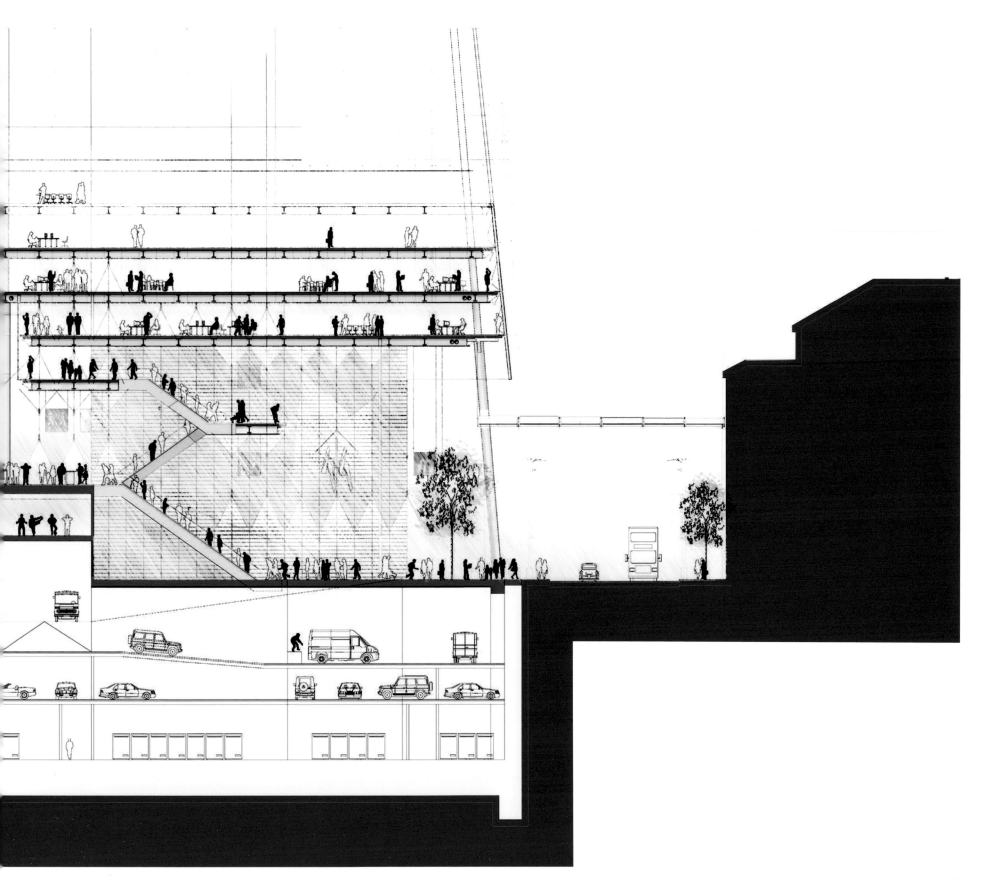

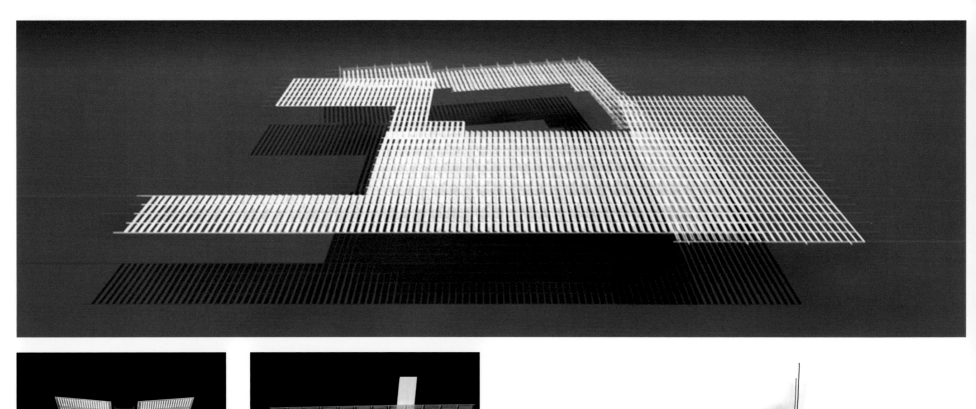

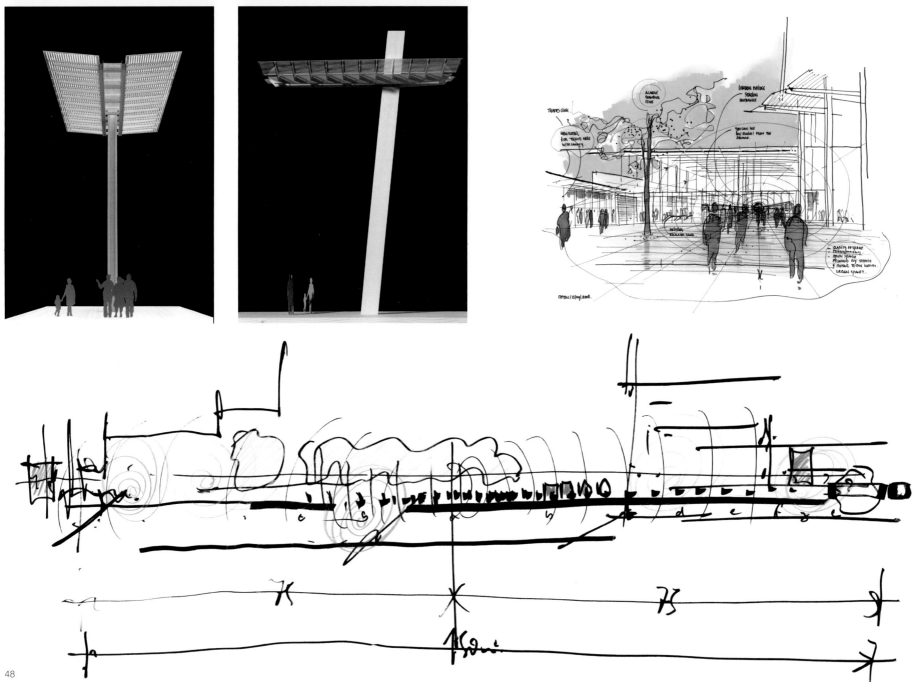

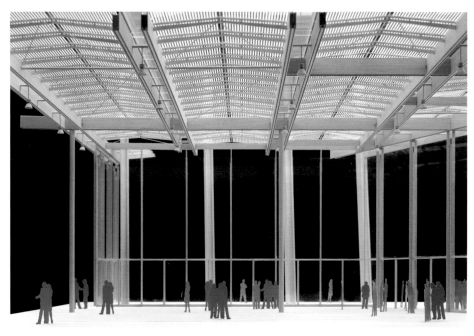

.....

Abbiamo coniugato questo sito irregolare con l'idea di un edificio che doveva diventare più slanciato verso l'alto, e con il concetto delle schegge che non si toccano l'un l'altra, per frammentare la scala dell'edificio e riflettere la luce in maniera imprevedibile, contribuendo a ridurre la presenza dello Shard nel cielo. Durante le prime presentazioni del progetto abbiamo usato immagini di camuffamento (come il *dazzle painting*) per rendere bene la nostra idea. Già dalla fase iniziale sapevamo di voler lavorare con una facciata di vetro, perché questo ci avrebbe dato maggiori possibilità di ottenere quell'effetto cristallino e immateriale che avrebbe potuto giocare con la luce e l'umore del tempo. RPBW aveva già lavorato molto con le facciate a doppia pelle per gli edifici più alti sulla Potsdamer Platz a Berlino, e anche per l'Aurora Place, una torre residenziale a Sydney. Ma la geometria e la grande altezza dello Shard non ci permettevano di applicare esattamente gli stessi principi, ad esempio l'intercapedine sulla facciata non poteva essere larga 600 mm e accessibile, perché avrebbe occupato troppo spazio. Conseguentemente abbiamo optato per un'intercapedine con una larghezza di 200 mm, sufficiente a installarvi all'interno una tenda avvolgibile. Naturalmente volevamo costruire un edificio dotato di caratteristiche eccezionali in termini di risparmio energetico: era un nostro dovere, soprattutto per un edificio di rilievo in una città che vanta, a buon diritto, di essere all'avanguardia nell'edilizia sostenibile. La logica della doppia facciata è molto semplice: le tende esterne mantengono efficacemente il calore solare all'esterno dell'edificio. In assenza di luce solare diretta, le tende sono avvolte e la facciata interamente in vetro massimizza la luce diurna naturale, riducendo la necessità di ricorrere all'illuminazione artificiale. Tuttavia, le tende esterne non sarebbero state una soluzione ottimale su un edificio alto: per questo abbiamo aggiunto un vetro singolo esterno, che crea un ambiente protetto per le tende e una ventilazione naturale che disperde il calore in eccesso. Ciò ci permette anche di utilizzare il vetro extra-white che conferisce alla torre il suo colore cristallino: questo vetro, infatti, contiene ossido di ferro in misura ridotta, il composto che conferisce il caratteristico colore verde al vetro comune. E basta guardarsi intorno per vedere cosa intendo: Londra è piena di edifici color verde bottiglia! Ma noi non potevamo accettarlo per una torre che spicca così sullo skyline di Londra. L'ispettore incaricato della Public Inquiry ha capito chiaramente l'importanza di questo dettaglio, che è stato integrato nelle condizioni per la concessione del permesso edilizio. Ma tornerò a parlare della facciata più avanti.
J.M.

.....

.....

We combined this irregular site and the idea of the building getting slenderer at the top with the concept of shards or facets which do not touch one another.
This would fragment the scale of the building and reflect the light in an unpredictable manner, thereby diminishing the presence of the entire building in the sky.
We showed dazzle paintings as one of our references in early presentations of the project. So from a very early stage we knew that we wanted to work with a glass facade as this would give us the best chance of achieving an immaterial, crystalline effect that would play with the light and the mood of the weather.
At RPBW we had worked extensively with double skin facades for the taller buildings at Potsdamer Platz in Berlin, and for Aurora Place, a residential tower in Sydney.
The geometry and the sheer height of the London tower would not allow us to apply exactly the same principles here, for example the facade cavity could not be 600 mm wide and accessible as this would lose us too much floor area. So we settled on a cavity in the range of 200 mm deep, enough to install a roller blind inside.
Of course we wanted to build a building with outstanding energy saving credentials; it is our duty particularly for such a high profile building in a city that prides itself rightly for being at the forefront of sustainable building practice.
The logic of the double facade is very simple: external blinds are highly effective in keeping solar heat gain out of the building. When there is no direct sunlight the blinds are rolled up and the fully glazed facade maximises natural daylight on the floors, reducing the use of artificial lighting. However, unprotected external blinds are not a very good idea on a tall building. This is where the additional layer of external single glazing comes into play, forming a protected environment for the blinds, with natural ventilation for the excess heat. This also allows us to use extra white glass which gives the building its crystalline character. This glass is low in iron oxide which gives the distinctive green colour in standard glass. Once you are aware of this and you walk through the city you can see exactly what this means: there are a lot of bottle green buildings around!
We could not accept this for a tower which is so prominent on the London skyline. The inspector of the Public Inquiry clearly understood the importance of this detail, and this point was incorporated into the conditions for granting planning permission. I will come back to the facade in further detail later on.
J.M.

.....

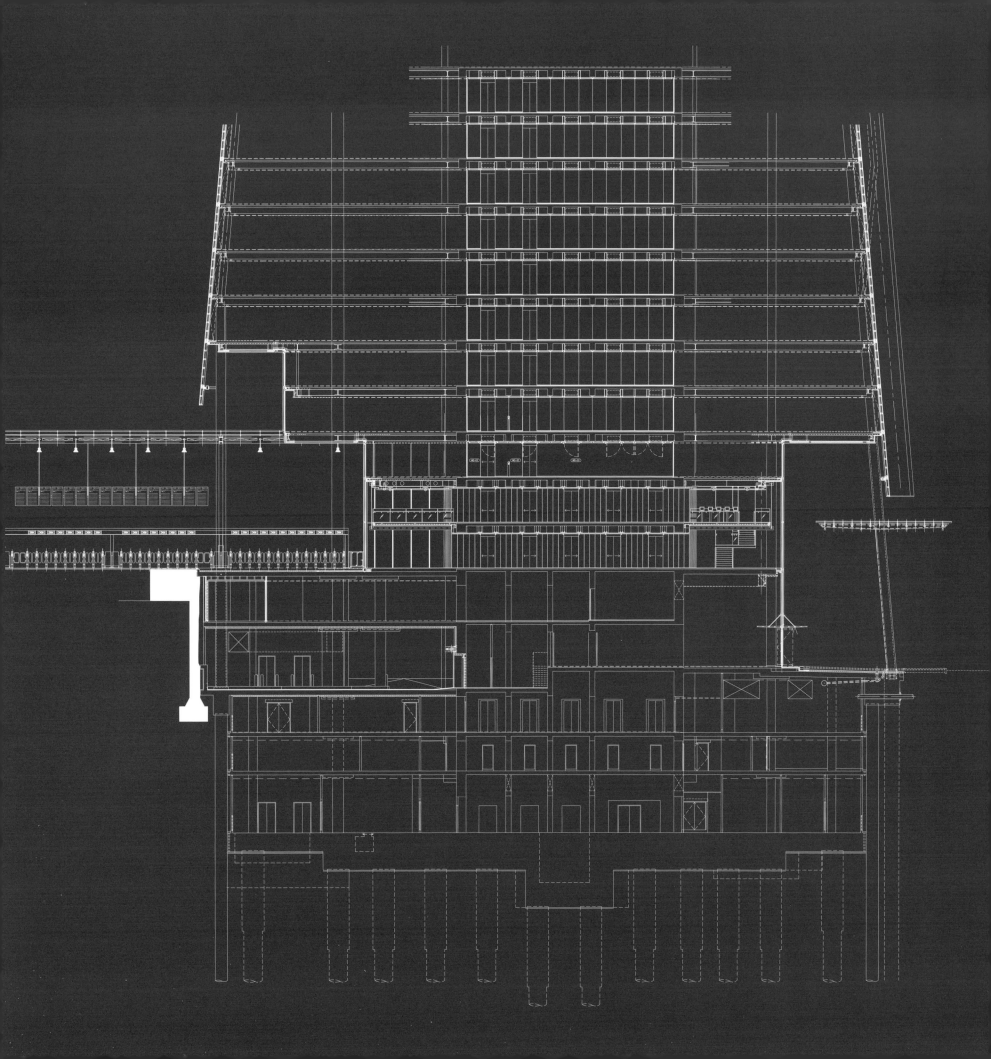

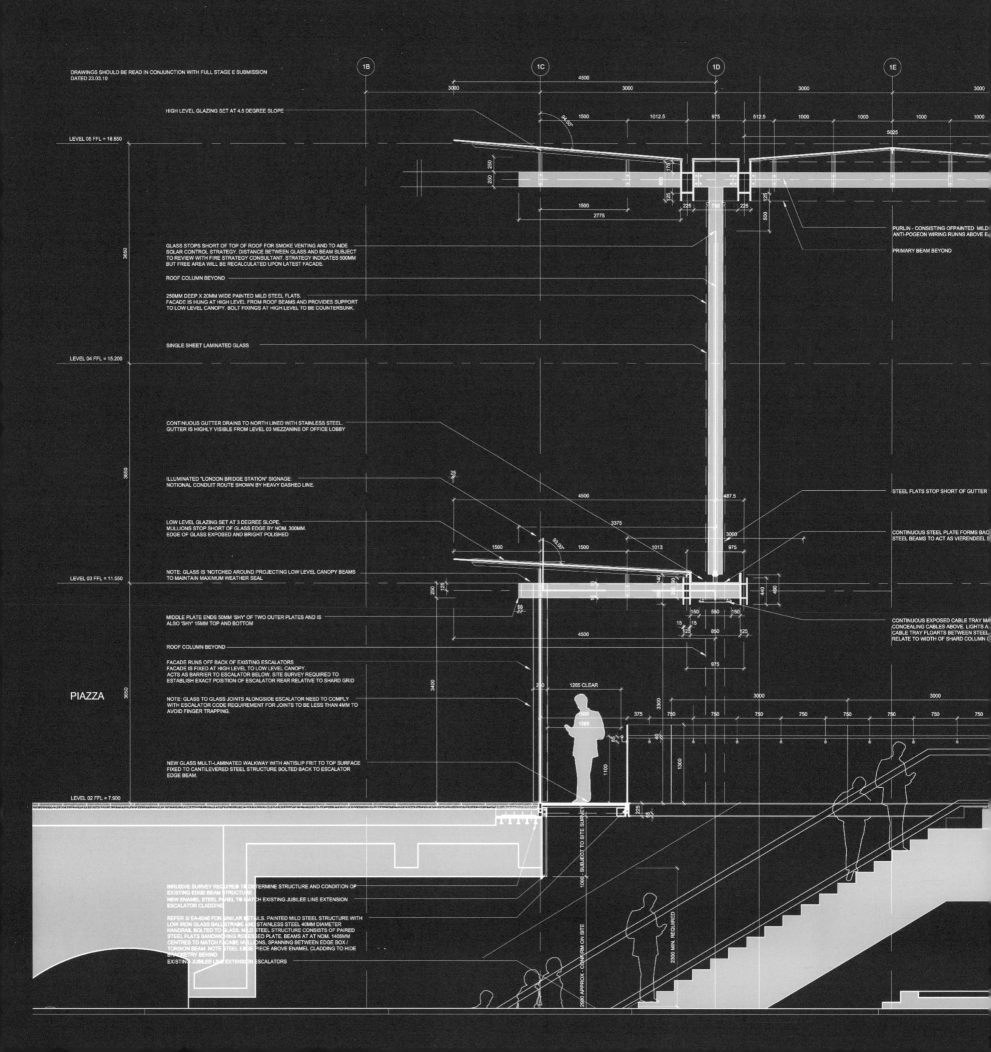

1B   1C   1D   1E

4500

3000   3000   3000   3000

HIGH LEVEL GLAZING SET AT 4.5 DEGREE SLOPE

1500   1012.5   975   512.5   1000   1000   1000

LEVEL 05 FFL = 18.850

94.50°

5025

250

250

175

680

PURLIN - CONSISTING OFPAINTED MILD
ANTI-POGEON WIRING RUNNS ABOVE E.

125   225   750   225   125   500   125

PRIMARY BEAM BEYOND

1500

2775

GLASS STOPS SHORT OF TOP OF ROOF FOR SMOKE VENTING AND TO AIDE
SOLAR CONTROL STRATEGY. DISTANCE BETWEEN GLASS AND BEAM SUBJECT
TO REVIEW WITH FIRE STRATEGY CONSULTANT. STRATEGY INDICATES 500MM
BUT FREE AREA WILL BE RECALCULATED UPON LATEST FACADE.

ROOF COLUMN BEYOND

250MM DEEP X 20MM WIDE PAINTED MILD STEEL FLATS.
FACADE IS HUNG AT HIGH LEVEL FROM ROOF BEAMS AND PROVIDES SUPPORT
TO LOW LEVEL CANOPY. BOLT FIXINGS AT HIGH LEVEL TO BE COUNTERSUNK.

SINGLE SHEET LAMINATED GLASS

LEVEL 04 FFL = 15.200

3650

CONTINUOUS GUTTER DRAINS TO NORTH LINED WITH STAINLESS STEEL.
GUTTER IS HIGHLY VISIBLE FROM LEVEL 03 MEZZANINE OF OFFICE LOBBY

25

487.5

STEEL FLATS STOP SHORT OF GUTTER

ILLUMINATED "LONDON BRIDGE STATION" SIGNAGE:
NOTIONAL CONDUIT ROUTE SHOWN BY HEAVY DASHED LINE.

4500

3375

3000

975

CONTINUOUS STEEL PLATE FORMS BAC
STEEL BEAMS TO ACT AS VIERENDEEL S

LOW LEVEL GLAZING SET AT 3 DEGREE SLOPE.
MULLIONS STOP SHORT OF GLASS EDGE BY NOM. 300MM.
EDGE OF GLASS EXPOSED AND BRIGHT POLISHED

63.00°

1500   1013   975

NOTE: GLASS IS 'NOTCHED AROUND PROJECTING LOW LEVEL CANOPY BEAMS
TO MAINTAIN MAXIMUM WEATHER SEAL

LEVEL 03 FFL = 11.550

250   125   140   440   490

MIDDLE PLATE ENDS 50MM 'SHY' OF TWO OUTER PLATES AND IS
ALSO 'SHY' 15MM TOP AND BOTTOM

50

150   550   150

15   15

125   850   125

CONTINUOUS EXPOSED CABLE TRAY MA
CONCEALING CABLES ABOVE. LIGHTS A
CABLE TRAY FLOARTS BETWEEN STEEL
RELATE TO WIDTH OF SHARD COLUMN (

ROOF COLUMN BEYOND

975

FACADE RUNS OFF BACK OF EXISTING ESCALATORS
FACADE IS FIXED AT HIGH LEVEL TO LOW LEVEL CANOPY.
ACTS AS BARRIER TO ESCALATOR BELOW. SITE SURVEY REQUIRED TO
ESTABLISH EXACT POSITION OF ESCALATOR REAR RELATIVE TO SHARD GRID

3650

PIAZZA

NOTE: GLASS TO GLASS JOINTS ALONGSIDE ESCALATOR NEED TO COMPLY
WITH ESCALATOR CODE REQUIREMENT FOR JOINTS TO BE LESS THAN 4MM TO
AVOID FINGER TRAPPING.

3400

250

1265 CLEAR

3300   3000   3000

375   750   750   750   750   750   750   750

500
1265

1100

1300

NEW GLASS MULTI-LAMINATED WALKWAY WITH ANTISLIP FRIT TO TOP SURFACE
FIXED TO CANTILEVERED STEEL STRUCTURE BOLTED BACK TO ESCALATOR
EDGE BEAM.

LEVEL 02 FFL = 7.900

225   55

INRUSIVE SURVEY REQUIRED TO DETERMINE STRUCTURE AND CONDITION OF
EXISTING EDGE BEAM STRUCTURE
NEW ENAMEL STEEL PANEL TO MATCH EXISTING JUBILEE LINE EXTENSION
ESCALATOR CLADDING

REFER 3/ EA-6046 FOR SIMILAR DETAILS. PAINTED MILD STEEL STRUCTURE WITH
LOW IRON GLASS BALUSTRADE AND STAINLESS STEEL 40MM DIAMETER
HANDRAIL BOLTED TO GLASS. MILD STEEL STRUCTURE CONSISTS OF PAIRED
STEEL FLATS SANDWICHING RECESSED PLATE. BEAMS AT AT NOM. 1408MM
CENTRES TO MATCH FACADE MULLIONS, SPANNING BETWEEN EDGE BOX /
TORSION BEAM. NOTE STEEL EDGE PIECE ABOVE ENAMEL CLADDING TO HIDE
BALCKETRY BEHIND.
EXISTING JUBILEE LINE EXTENSION ESCALATORS

1000 SUBJECT TO SITE SURVEY

2900 APPROX - CONFIRM ON SITE

2300 MIN REQUIRED

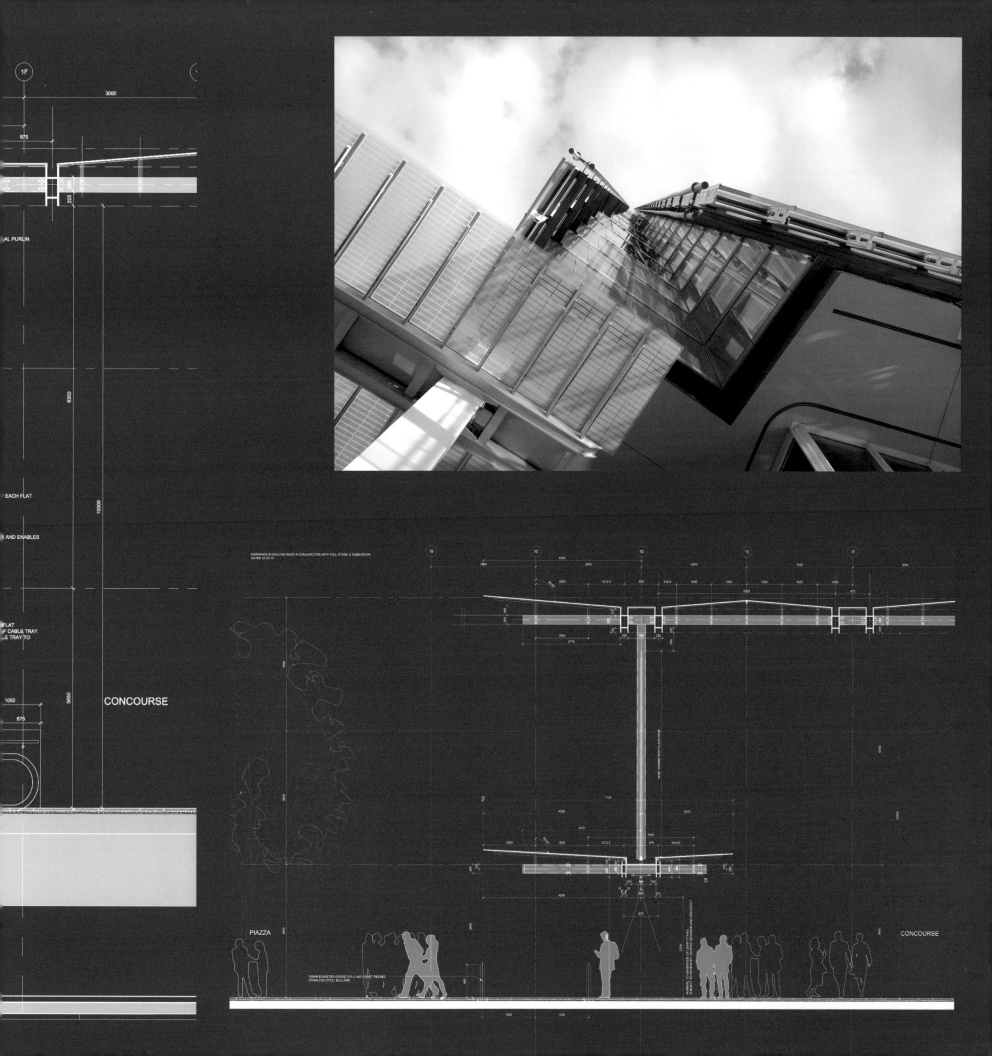

1F

3000

975

225 320

AL PURLIN

6350

10000

EACH FLAT

AND ENABLES

FLAT
F CABLE TRAY.
LE TRAY TO

3650

1050

CONCOURSE

675

DRAWINGS SHOULD BE READ IN CONJUNCTION WITH FULL STAGE E SUBMISSION DATED 23.03.10

1B   1C   1D   1E   1F

PIAZZA   CONCOURSE

125MM DIAMETER GRADE 316 (1.4401) SHOT PEENED
STAINLESS STEEL BOLLARD

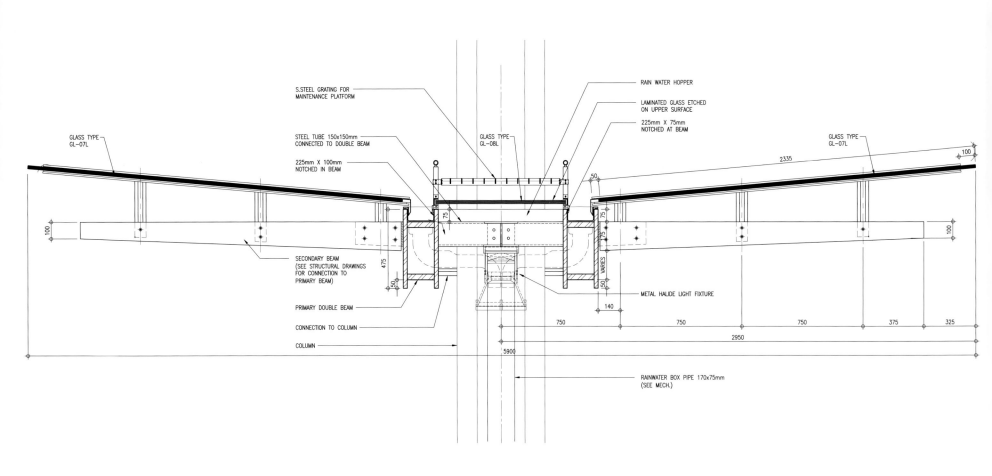

GLASS TYPE
GL-07L

S.STEEL GRATING FOR
MAINTENANCE PLATFORM

STEEL TUBE 150x150mm
CONNECTED TO DOUBLE BEAM

225mm X 100mm
NOTCHED IN BEAM

GLASS TYPE
GL-08L

RAIN WATER HOPPER

LAMINATED GLASS ETCHED
ON UPPER SURFACE

225mm X 75mm
NOTCHED AT BEAM

GLASS TYPE
GL-07L

SECONDARY BEAM
(SEE STRUCTURAL DRAWINGS
FOR CONNECTION TO
PRIMARY BEAM)

PRIMARY DOUBLE BEAM

CONNECTION TO COLUMN

COLUMN

METAL HALIDE LIGHT FIXTURE

RAINWATER BOX PIPE 170x75mm
(SEE MECH.)

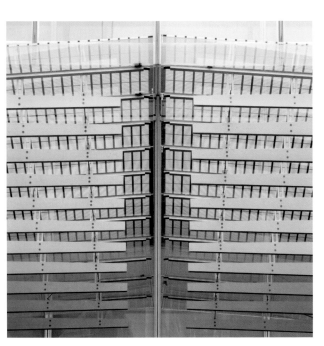

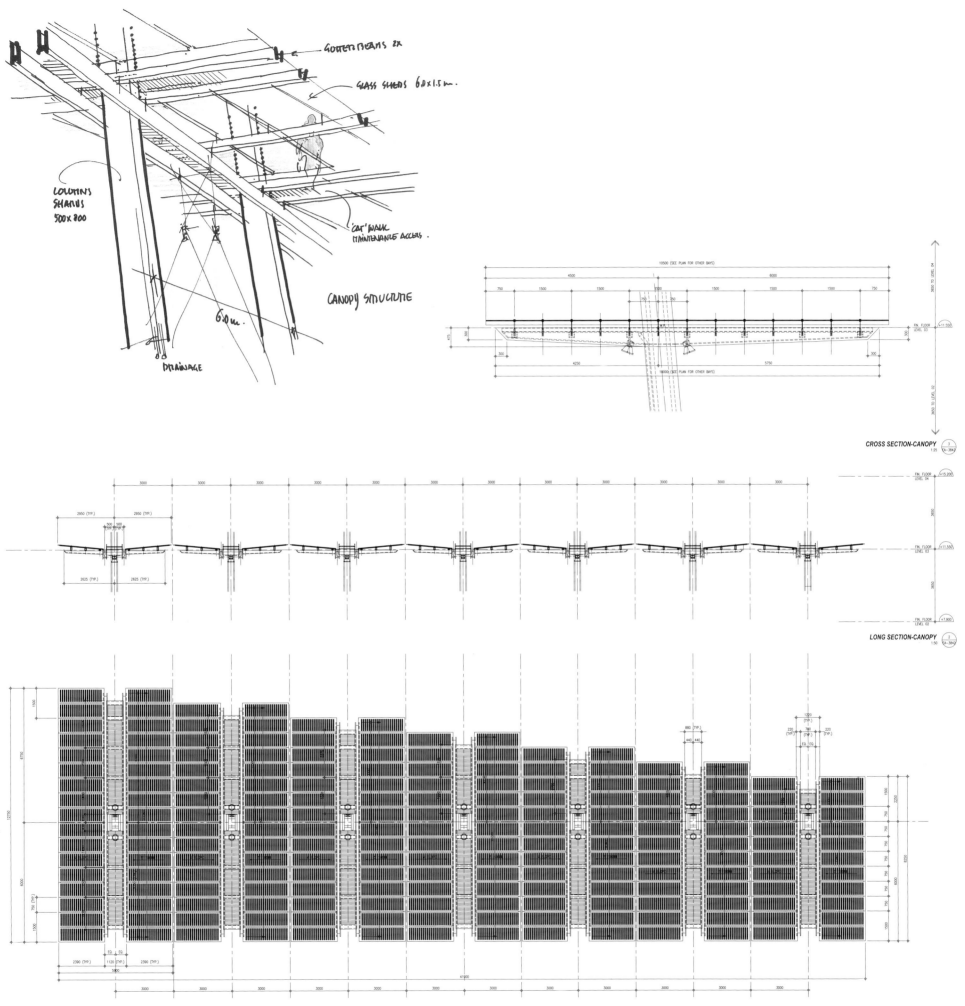

GOTTER BEAMS 2x

GLASS SHEDS 6.0 x 1.5 m.

COLUMNS SHAFTS 500 x 800

'CAT' WALK MAINTENANCE ACCESS.

DRAINAGE

6.0 m.

CANOPY STRUCTURE

CROSS SECTION-CANOPY

LONG SECTION-CANOPY

.....

Torniamo, nel dettaglio, allo sviluppo della facciata. La complessa geometria della torre ha decisamente rappresentato una sfida per noi. Sarebbe stato possibile un tradizionale sistema di facciate, piuttosto che ricorrere all'assemblaggio di singoli pezzi? Siamo riusciti a convincere Sellar che sarebbe stato utile lavorare sin dalla prima fase del progetto (Fase D RIBA) con un selezionato gruppo di contraenti specializzati in facciate. L'idea è stata quindi ulteriormente sviluppata, e sin dall'inizio della Fase E RIBA, abbiamo lavorato in ottemperanza a un PCSA (Pre-Contract Service Agreement, un Accordo di Servizio Pre-Contrattuale) con un unico appaltatore, Permasteelisa-Scheldebouw. Mentre il cliente desiderava mantenere la concorrenza tra gli appaltatori, noi per realizzare un edificio con un sistema di facciate così sofisticato volevamo il contributo di uno specialista sin dall'incipit del processo di progettazione. La posta in gioco era alta dal punto di vista della progettazione, perché durante la Public Inquiry avevamo fatto precise promesse, letteralmente sotto giuramento, in merito alla facciata. Ancora una volta, Irvine Sellar ha avuto fiducia in noi e ci ha concesso la libertà (entro limiti definiti) di esplorare e sviluppare la soluzione migliore. È interessante vedere come si evolvono le cose: alcune idee che all'inizio sembravano impossibili si sono rivelate fattibili, mentre altre, inizialmente immediate, sono diventate un ostacolo da superare per convincere tutti ad accettare. Fino alla Fase D (luglio 2005) avevamo in progetto una facciata attiva in cui il calore solare accumulato nell'intercapedine avrebbe potuto essere incanalato meccanicamente.

Questo sistema aveva il vantaggio di essere completamente protetto dagli elementi esterni, tuttavia presentava anche due svantaggi: un sistema meccanico ha bisogno di energia per funzionare, e i condotti nei soffitti e le alzate occupano molto spazio prezioso. All'inizio della Fase E RIBA abbiamo deciso di optare per una facciata passiva ventilata naturalmente verso l'esterno, con l'intercapedine accessibile dalle piattaforme per la pulizia della facciata. Il vantaggio maggiore per gli appartamenti privati e l'hotel è che non serve passare dall'interno per la manutenzione. Su questa base abbiamo costruito con Scheldebouw un modello in scala ridotta presso il nostro laboratorio a Genova, che un'enorme gru teneva sospeso a 30 metri di altezza mentre lo giravamo per capire l'effetto visivo della doppia facciata e del trattamento del vetro. Con le panoramiche verificate obbligatorie e le immagini di sintesi, abbiamo simulato varie opzioni e capito che un vetro riflettente al 20% costituiva la soluzione migliore. Queste immagini sono state quindi utilizzate come prova per la richiesta di Concessione Edilizia e la Public Inquiry. Per il progetto reale era chiaro che avremmo dovuto trovare un vetro dal medesimo effetto. Il vetro Antelio di Saint Gobain ci si avvicinava, ma non potevamo usarlo sopra il vetro extra-white che desideravamo. Successivamente, Interpane ha sviluppato con noi Ipasol

Bright specificamente per lo Shard: potrebbe sembrare tutto semplice e immediato, ma sono servite molte prove all'esterno del nostro ufficio con diverse combinazioni di circa 40 campioni prima di ottenere il risultato giusto. Oggi il vetro è un prodotto altamente tecnico, ma selezionare e manipolare le diverse opzioni rimane sempre una forma di arte. Le discussioni con il cliente ci hanno portato al terzo e ultimo passo nello sviluppo del progetto della facciata. Abbiamo seguito la logica di una facciata con ventilazione naturale, tramite un ingegnoso sistema di guarnizioni poste tra i montanti verticali, ma abbiamo abbandonato l'idea dell'accesso esterno all'intercapedine per la pulizia e la manutenzione, permettendo invece di aprire da dentro il pannello interno, mentre quello esterno rimane fisso. Inoltre abbiamo progettato un sistema di montanti sovrapposti, che facessero da ponte con l'intercapedine per fare sembrare la facciata quanto più leggera possibile. Un ulteriore dettaglio, tanto piccolo quanto importante: il pannello esterno è realizzato in vetro float, un tipo di vetro estremamente piano, mentre quello temperato presenta frequentemente una caratteristica ondulazione. Questo è importante perché conferisce allo Shard la sua caratteristica finezza e precisione, e significa che i riflessi in cielo e sulle nuvole non sono soggetti a distorsioni come invece succede per molti altri edifici in vetro. Per verificare questo sistema, nel febbraio del 2009 abbiamo costruito un modello in scala reale presso lo stabilimento Scheldebouw in Olanda, dove abbiamo anche testato i dettagli dei muri perimetrali, le estremità a sbalzo dei piani facciata, che servono per dar forma alle schegge, con sbalzi compresi tra 1,5 m e 3,5 m, alcuni addirittura fino a 4,2 m. Dal momento che abbiamo usato solo vetro extra-white, il valore G è pari a 0,55, e ciò significa che il 55% del calore solare penetra all'interno dell'edificio: questo, naturalmente, non è positivo, ma con le tende abbassate (5% di trasmissione della luce), il valore G scende a un eccellente 0,12. Le tende sono gestite automaticamente da un Sistema di Gestione dell'Edificio (BMS – Building Management System) monitorato da una stazione meteo per ciascuna delle 8 schegge. I primi test sulla facciata, come la resistenza all'acqua in condizioni di elevatissima pressione eolica provocata da un'elica per aeroplani e il test acustico completo, sono stati svolti nel mese di luglio del 2009. Il primo elemento unitario è stato installato in loco nel maggio del 2010. In totale la facciata è composta da 11.000 elementi installati con una media di 200 a settimana. La ragione per cui non si vedono griglie di ventilazione sulle facciate dello Shard è che le abbiamo nascoste all'interno delle fratture presenti tre le schegge. I vani macchine sono appena visibili, perché abbiamo provveduto a utilizzare la medesima doppia facciata, in cui il pannello interno è opaco e di colore grigio scuro. Ciò ha permesso di garantire che la continuità delle schegge dall'alto in basso non fosse visivamente interrotta da una cintura di piani adibiti a contenimento macchine. Durante una delle prime visite

al cantiere, in fase di demolizione delle Southwark Towers, abbiamo fatto una passeggiata con Renzo che ha suggerito di inserire del colore nel progetto. Abbiamo considerato varie opzioni che sarebbero rientrate nei parametri della Public Inquiry e abbiamo deciso di usare il colore per gli alloggiamenti delle tende che sono posizionati appena sotto il davanzale di ogni pannello nell'intercapedine della facciata. Abbiamo testato il sistema sul nostro ultimo modello usando una calda tonalità di rosso aranciato e abbiamo avviato la produzione… Mesi più tardi, una volta installato un buon numero di piani, Irvine Sellar ha chiamato William Matthews chiedendogli quando sarebbe stata tolta la pellicola arancione di protezione dagli alloggiamenti delle tende. Naturalmente non era possibile! La cosa interessante è che questi alloggiamenti si vedono a malapena nei mesi estivi, quando il sole è alto e rimangono nascosti all'ombra dei davanzali. Tuttavia, nei mesi invernali, quando il sole è basso e li colpisce direttamente, l'edificio sfodera un caldo bagliore dorato.

J.M.

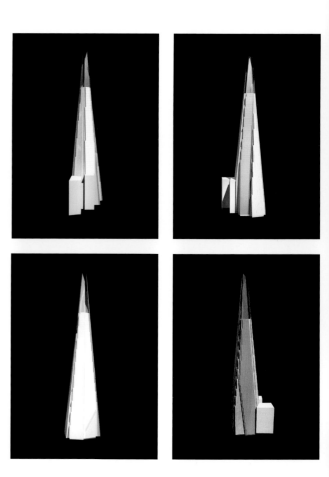

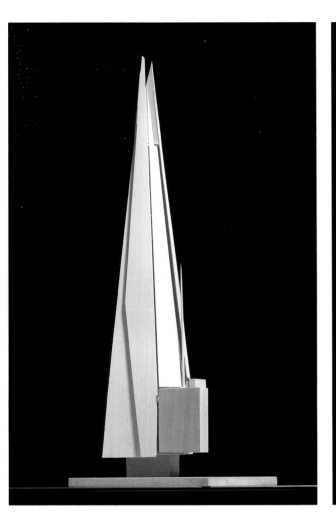
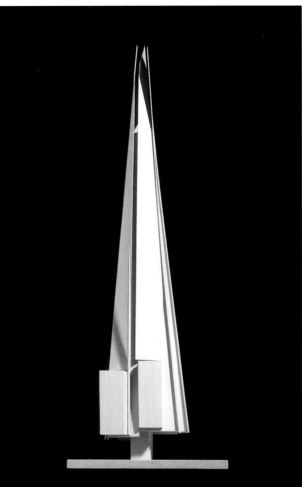
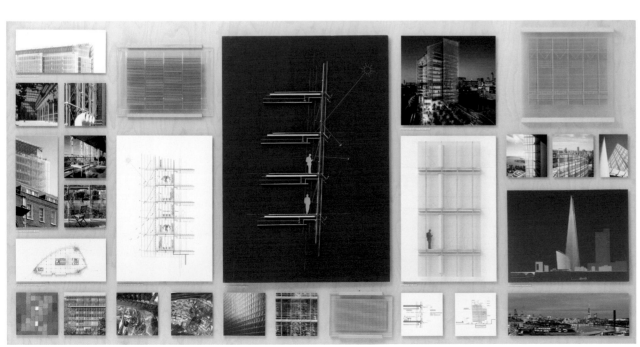

.....

Let us go back to the facade development in further detail: The complex geometry of the tower was admittedly a challenge for us. Would it be possible to apply a regular unitised facade system, rather than having to make lots of unique pieces? We managed to convince Sellar that it would be beneficial to work from the early design development stage (RIBA Stage D) with a select group of facade contractors. This idea was developed further, and from the beginning of RIBA Stage E we worked under a PCSA (Pre-Contract Service Agreement) with only one contractor, Permasteelisa-Scheldebouw. Whilst the client understandably wanted to keep contractors working in a competitive commercial environment we wanted the input of a specialist contractor early on in the design process for such a tall building with a sophisticated façade system. The stakes were high from our design perspective because during the Public Inquiry we had made specific promises about the façade, literally under oath. Here again Irvine Sellar put his trust in us and gave us the freedom (within agreed boundaries) to explore and develop the right solution. It is interesting to see how things evolve - some ideas that seemed impossible at the start turned out to be quite feasible while others that were initially straightforward became a hurdle to solve or to convince everyone to agree on. Until Stage D (July 2005) we had designed an active façade where accumulated solar heat in the cavity would be extracted mechanically via ducts. This facade system had the advantage of being completely protected from external elements but also two significant disadvantages: a mechanical system uses energy to operate and the ducts in the ceilings and risers take valuable lettable space. At the start of RIBA Stage E, we decided to change to a passive façade naturally ventilated to the exterior and with the cavity accessed from the façade cleaning cradle.

The advantage is that you do not have to enter the tenants' floors for maintenance, notably for the private apartments and the hotel. On this basis we built a full-scale mock-up with Scheldebouw at our workshop in Voltri, a couple of kilometres from our Genoa office. A large crane hoisted the entire mock-up 30m in the air while turning it so we could understand the visual effects of the double facade and the glass treatment.

For the obligatory verified views / Computer Generated Images we simulated various optionas and realised that 20% reflectivity was the right choice. The images were then used for the Planning Application and the Public Inquiry as proof of evidence. For the real project it was clear to us that we had to find a glass with the same effect. Saint Gobain's Antelio glass came close but could not be used on extra white glass which we wanted.

Interpane then developed Ipasol Bright with us specifically for the Shard. This may all sound easy and fast, however it took us many tests outside our office with many different combinations of around 40 samples to get right.

Glass is now a highly technical product but selecting and manipulating the different options remains an art form. Discussions with the client with the aim of reducing risk to a minimum made us take the third and final step in the design development of the facade.

We kept the logic of a naturally ventilated façade, through an ingenious system of ventilation gaskets between the vertical mullions, but abandoned the external access to the cavity for cleaning and maintenance. We made the inner leaf, the Double Glazed Unit, now openable from the inside and the outer pane fixed. We also designed a castellated mullion system, bridging the cavity to make the facade appear as light as possible. Finally, another small but very important detail, the outer leaf comprises laminated float glass and not toughened.

Float glass is extremely flat, whilst toughened glass frequently has a distinctive roller wave. This is important because it gives the Shard its sharp and precise quality and means that reflections of the sky and clouds are not subject to the distortions you see on many other glazed buildings. To check this system in February 2009 we built a further full-scale mock-up at the Scheldebouw facility in Holland. Here we also tested the detailing of the wing walls, the cantilevered edges of the façade planes. We have the wing walls to express the shape of the shards, with cantilevers between 1.5 m and 3.5 m and some even up to 4.2 m. As we used only extra white glass, the G value is 0.55, meaning 55% of the solar heat gets transmitted inside the building, which is of course not good, but with the blinds down (5% light transmittance), the G value drops to only 0.12, which is excellent.

The blinds are deployed automatically by the BMS (Building Management System) monitored by a weather station point for each of the 8 shards. The first facade tests, including a water penetration test under very high wind pressure using a aeroplane propeller/engine installation and a full acoustic test, were carried out in July 2009. The first unitised element was installed on site in May 2010. In total we had 11,000 facade elements installed at an average of 200 per week.

The reason why you do not see any ventilation grilles on the Shard facades is that we have hidden them in what we call the fractures between the shards. The plant rooms are only notionally visible as we made sure that the same double facade was used, with the inner pane replaced by a dark grey opaque panel. This was to ensure that the continuity of the shards from top to bottom is not visually interrupted by a belt of plant room floors.

During one of our early site visits when Southwark Towers was being demolished we had a walk around with Renzo and he mentioned we should introduce colour to the scheme. We looked at various options which would stay within the parameters of the Public Inquiry and decided to use colour for the blind boxes which are housed just under the sill of each panel in the facade cavity.

We tested this on our last mock-up with a warm orange red colour and it went into production... Months later when a good number of floors were already installed Irvine Sellar called William asking when the protective orange film would be taken off the blind boxes. Of course this was not possible! The interesting thing about these boxes is that they are hardly visible in the summer months when the sun is high and they remain in the shadow of the sills. However in the winter months with a low sun shining directly onto them the building gets a warm red glow. J.M.

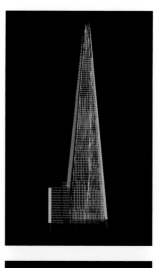

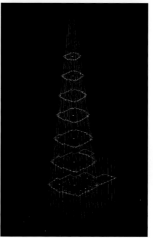

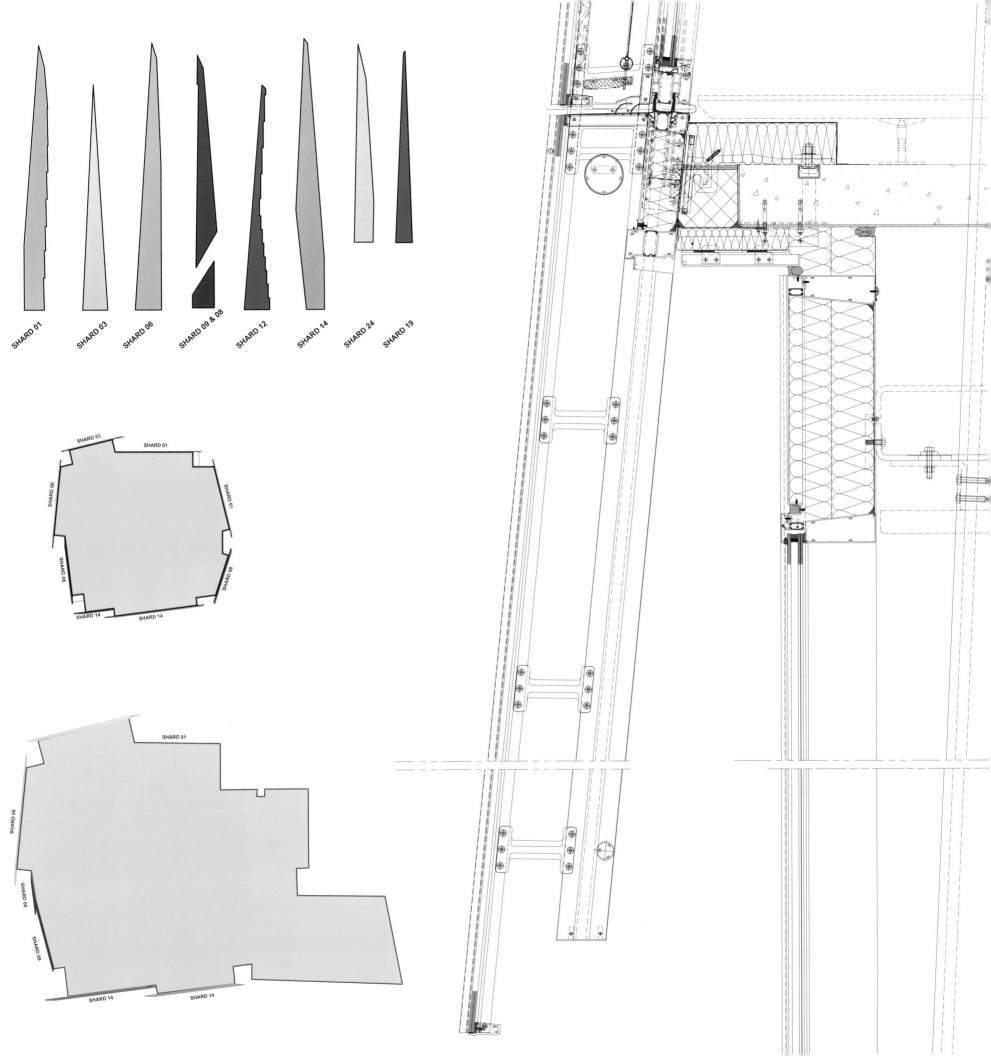

SHARD 01 SHARD 03 SHARD 06 SHARD 09 & 08 SHARD 12 SHARD 14 SHARD 24 SHARD 19

SHARD 03
SHARD 01
SHARD 06
SHARD 01
SHARD 08
SHARD 08
SHARD 14
SHARD 14

SHARD 01
SHARD 06
SHARD 06
SHARD 09
SHARD 14
SHARD 14

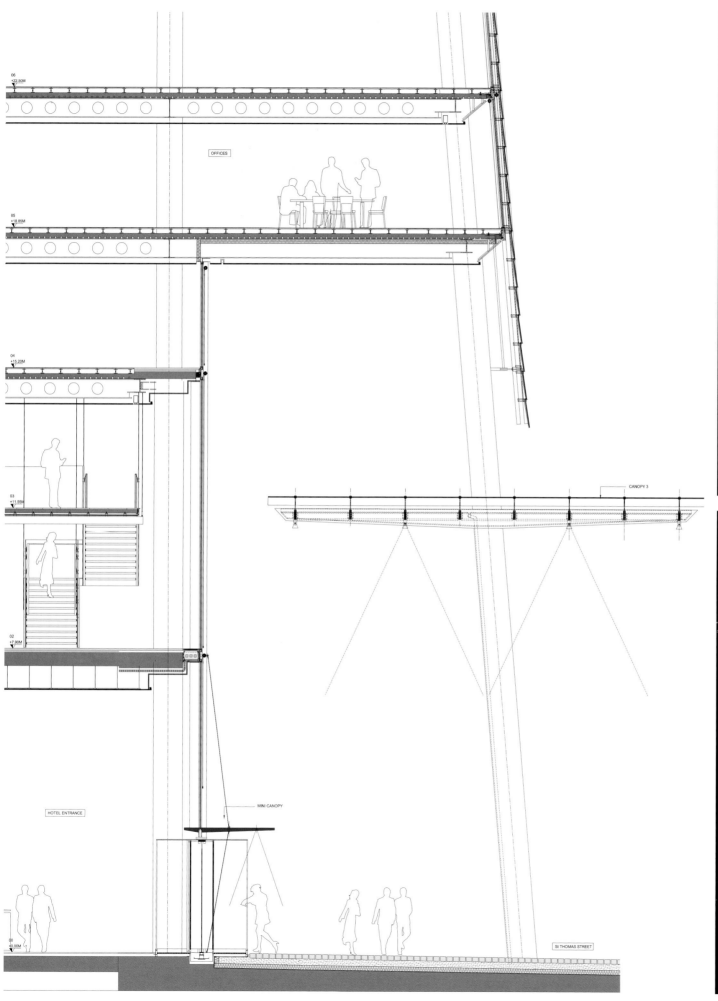

06
+22.50M

OFFICES

05
+18.85M

04
+15.20M

03
+11.55M

CANOPY 3

02
+7.90M

HOTEL ENTRANCE

MINI CANOPY

St THOMAS STREET

00
±0.00M

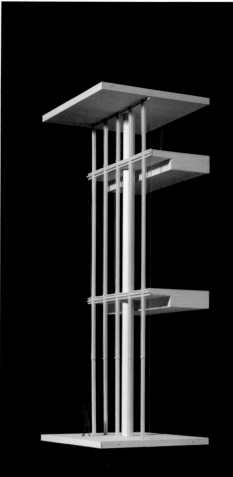

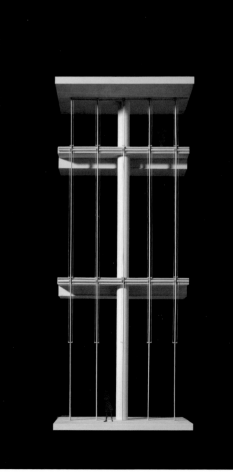

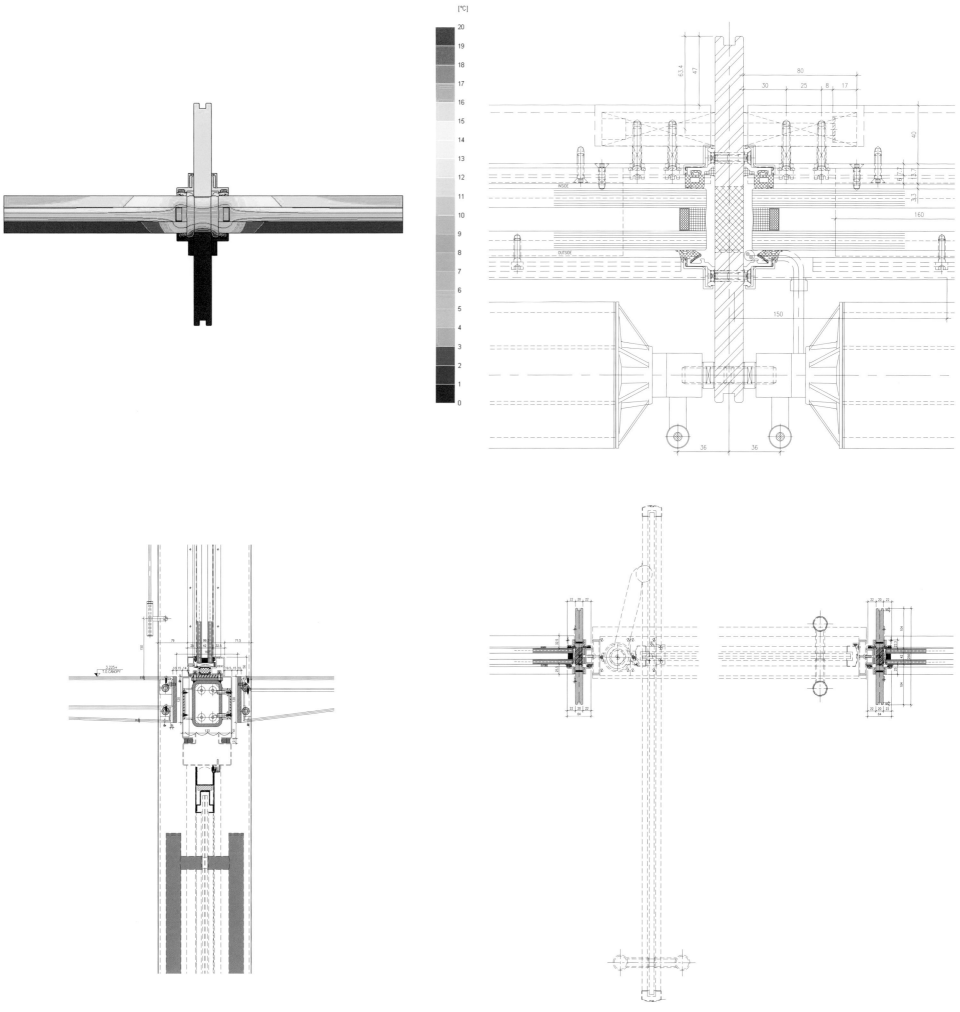

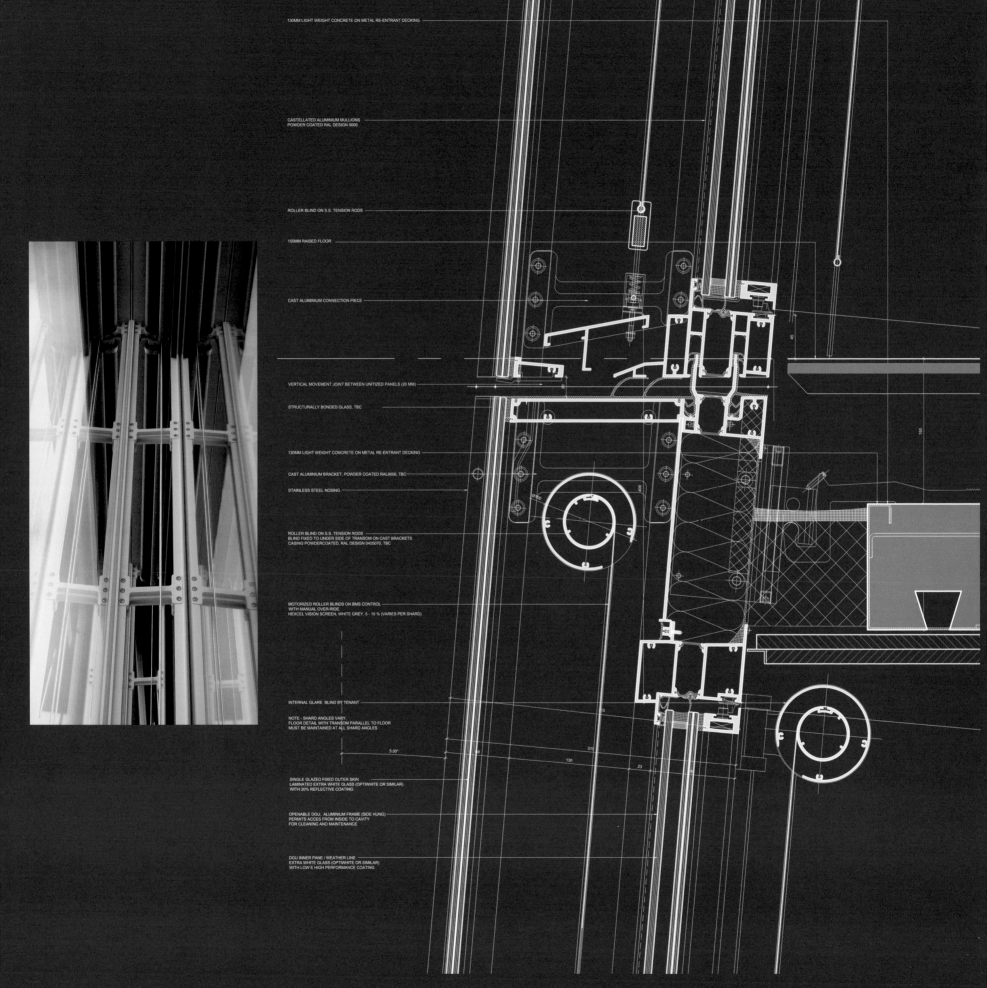

130MM LIGHT WEIGHT CONCRETE ON METAL RE-ENTRANT DECKING

CASTELLATED ALUMINIUM MULLIONS
POWDER COATED RAL DESIGN 9000

ROLLER BLIND ON S.S. TENSION RODS

150MM RAISED FLOOR

CAST ALUMINIUM CONNECTION PIECE

VERTICAL MOVEMENT JOINT BETWEEN UNITIZED PANELS (20 MM)

STRUCTURALLY BONDED GLASS, TBC

130MM LIGHT WEIGHT CONCRETE ON METAL RE-ENTRANT DECKING

CAST ALUMINIUM BRACKET, POWDER COATED RAL9006, TBC

STAINLESS STEEL NOSING

ROLLER BLIND ON S.S. TENSION RODS
BLIND FIXED TO UNDER SIDE OF TRANSOM ON CAST BRACKETS
CASING POWDERCOATED, RAL DESIGN 0405070, TBC

MOTORIZED ROLLER BLINDS ON BMS CONTROL
WITH MANUAL OVER-RIDE.
HEXCEL VISION SCREEN, WHITE GREY, 5 - 10 % (VARIES PER SHARD)

INTERNAL GLARE BLIND BY TENANT

NOTE - SHARD ANGLES VARY.
FLOOR DETAIL WITH TRANSOM PARALLEL TO FLOOR
MUST BE MAINTAINED AT ALL SHARD ANGLES

5.00°

SINGLE GLAZED FIXED OUTER SKIN
LAMINATED EXTRA WHITE GLASS (OPTIWHITE OR SIMILAR)
WITH 20% REFLECTIVE COATING.

OPENABLE DGU. ALUMINIUM FRAME (SIDE HUNG)
PERMITS ACCES FROM INSIDE TO CAVITY
FOR CLEANING AND MAINTENANCE

DGU INNER PANE / WEATHER LINE
EXTRA WHITE GLASS (OPTIWHITE OR SIMILAR)
WITH LOW E HIGH PERFORMANCE COATING

150MM RAISED FLOOR

130MM LIGHT WEIGHT CONCRETE ON METAL RE-ENTRANT DECKING

FIRE STOP DETAIL

ROLLER BLIND ON S.S. TENSION RODS
BLIND FIXED TO CAST BRACKETS

PERIMETER COLUMN ENCASED IN PREFABRICATED FIBROUS
PLASTER COLUMN CASING/FIRE PROOFING

70MM FIRE/TOLERANCE/DEFLECTION ZONE/
FIRE PROTECTION ASSUMED SPRAYED
= NOM. 25MM THICKNESS.
T.B.C. BY DETAILED STUDY

PERIMETER LINEAR SLOT DIFFUSER

CASTELLATED ALUMINIUM MULLIONS
POWDER COATED RAL DESIGN 9000

CAST ALUMINIUM CONNECTION PIECE

SINGLE GLAZED FIXED OUTER SKIN
LAMINATED EXTRA WHITE GLASS (OPTIWHITE OR SIMILAR)
WITH 24% REFLECTIVE COATING.

DGU INNER PANE / WEATHER LINE
OPENABLE FROM INTERIOR, SIDE HINGED
EXTRA WHITE GLASS (OPTIWHITE OR SIMILAR)
WITH LOW E HIGH PERFORMANCE COATING

TOP OF TRANSOM 45MM ABOVE FFL

FLOOR MOUNTED CLADDING BRACKET

MOTORIZED ROLLER BLINDS ON BMS CONTROL
WITH MANUAL OVER-RIDE.
HEXCEL VISION SCREEN, WHITE GREY. 5 - 10 % (VARIES PER SHARD)

500MM MAXIMUM BEAM DEPTH

NOTE - SHARD ANGLES VARY.
FLOOR DETAIL WITH TRANSOM PARALLEL TO FLOOR
MUST BE MAINTAINED AT ALL SHARD ANGLES

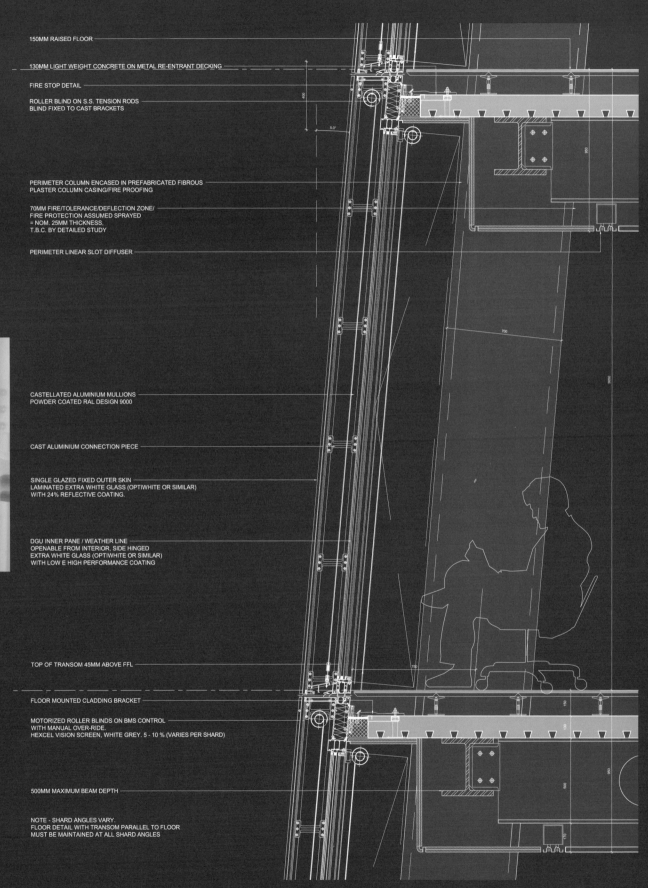

EXTERIOR PANE / INTERIOR PANE	DIAMANT - 0 %		ANTELIO - 30 %	
	6° - perpendicular	From below 30°	6° - perpendicular	From below 30°
LOW E - 10%	12:19	13:34	12:22	13:32
SKN 054 - 20%	12:26	13:30	12:29	13:28
ANTELIO 30 - 30%	12:33	13:24	12:36	13:23
IPASOL 30 - 30%	12:39	13:20	12:41	13:18
IPASOL 40 - 40%	12:45	13:14	12:49	13:12
KS 047 - 40 %	12:54	13:09	12:55	13:06

MOCK UP
06/12/06

RPBW

wheather : parlty cloudy

wheather : sunny, no direct sun

Location : 34 rue des archives, 75004 Paris

Lat : 48°51'32,54" N
Long: 2°21'21,17" E

Camera settings

Type : Canon EOS 400D
Lens : 17/85 mm
Mode : Manual 1/80 - F7,1

Type : Canon EOS 400D
Lens : 17/85 mm
Mode : Manual 1/125 - F11,0

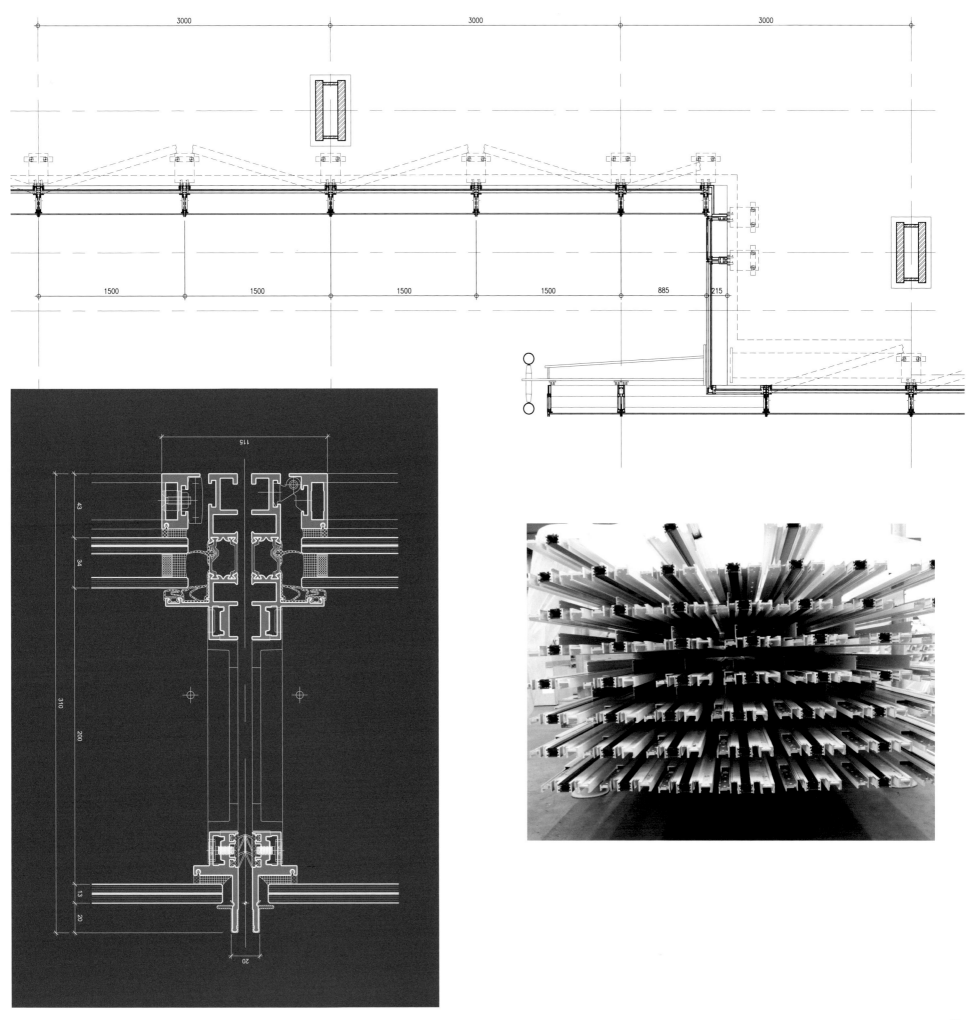

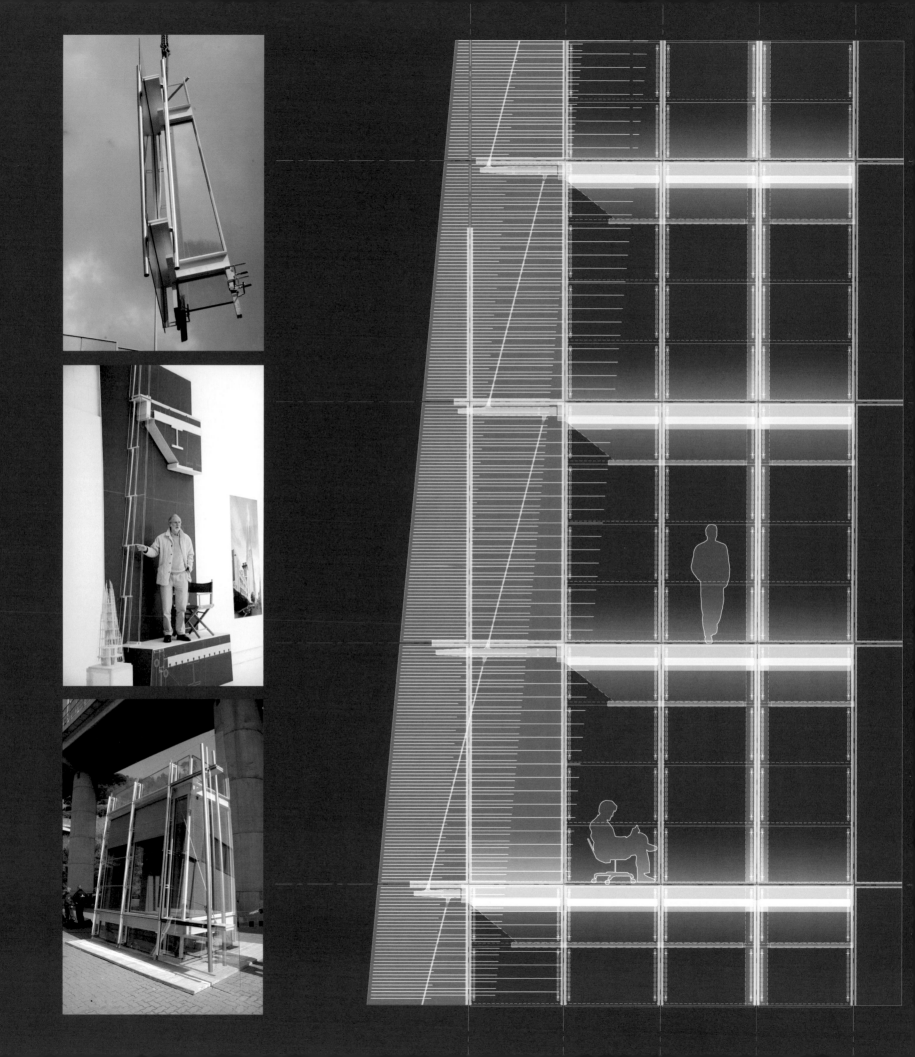

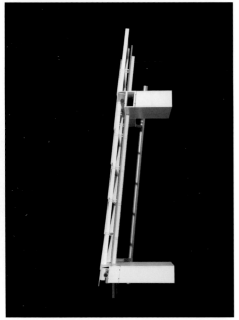

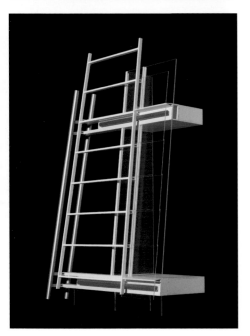

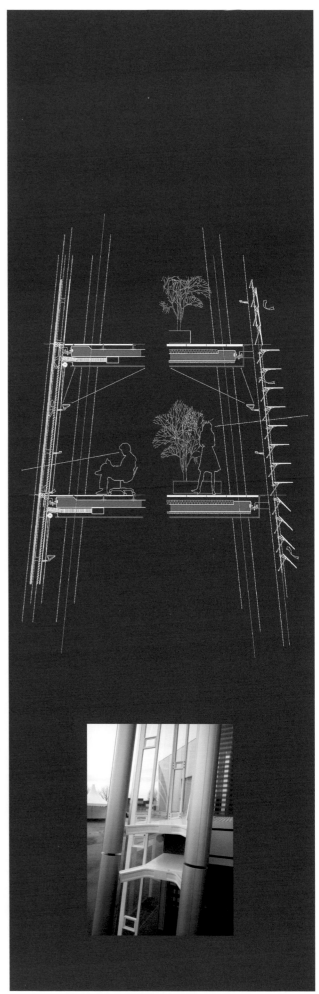

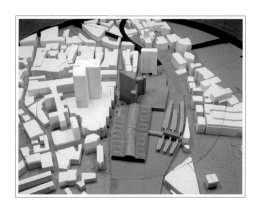

Wind Tunnel Study Model	Figure No.	1a	RWDI
Configuration A - Existing			
London Bridge Tower - London, United Kingdom Project #04-1514	Date: November 22, 2004		

Wind Tunnel Study Model	Figure No.	1b	RWDI
Configuration B - Proposed			
London Bridge Tower - London, United Kingdom Project #04-1514	Date: November 22, 2004		

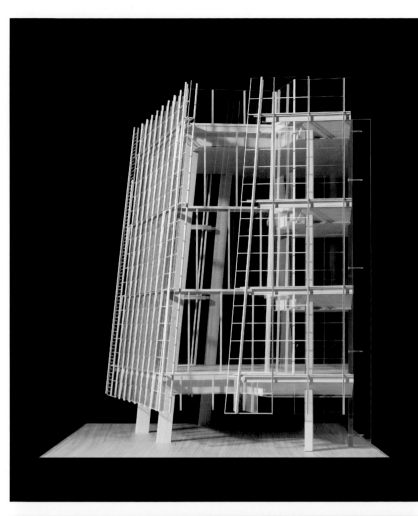

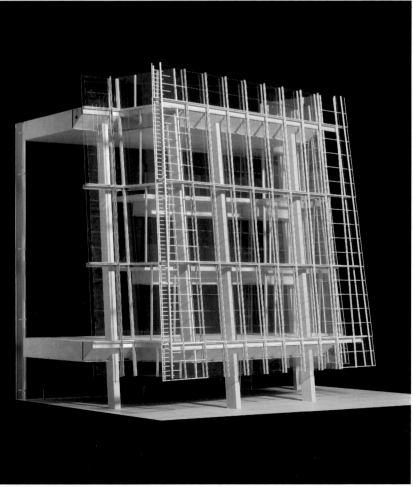

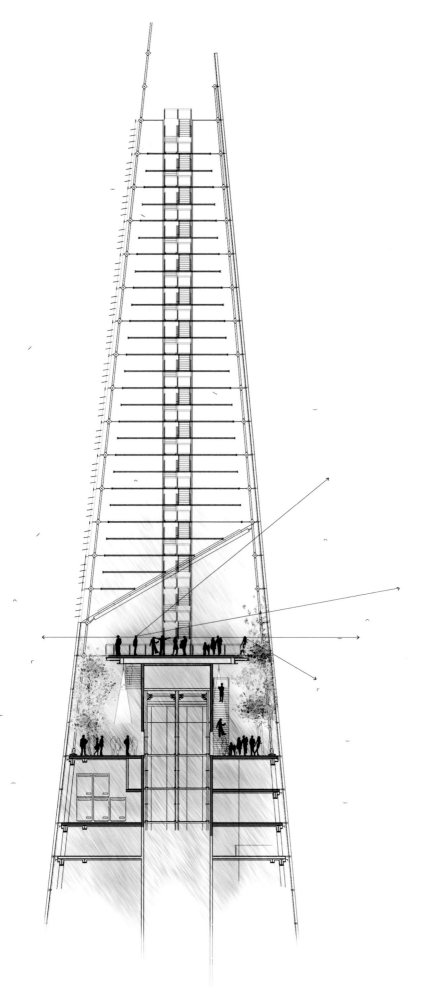
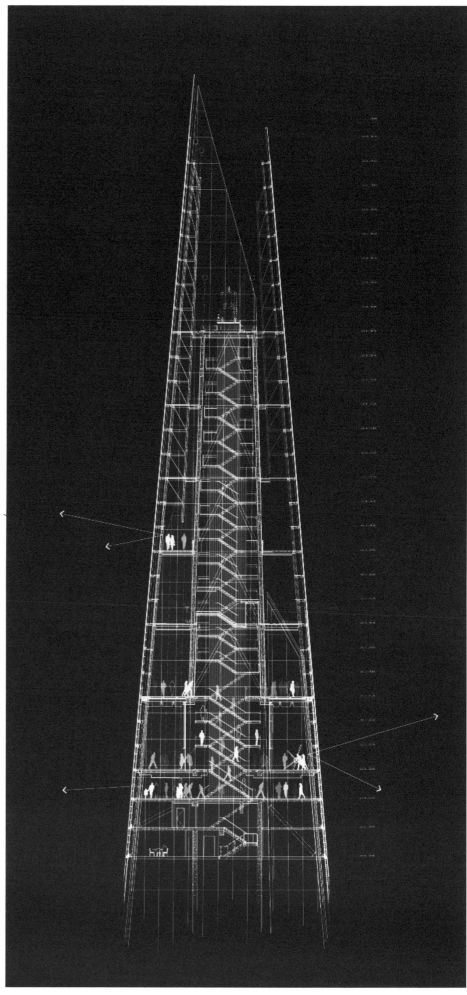

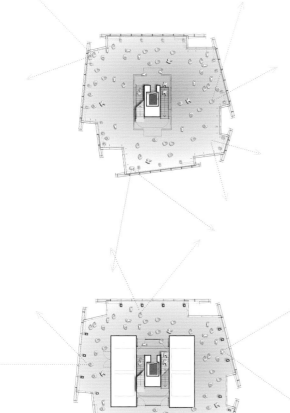

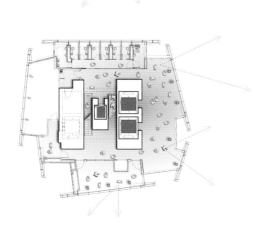

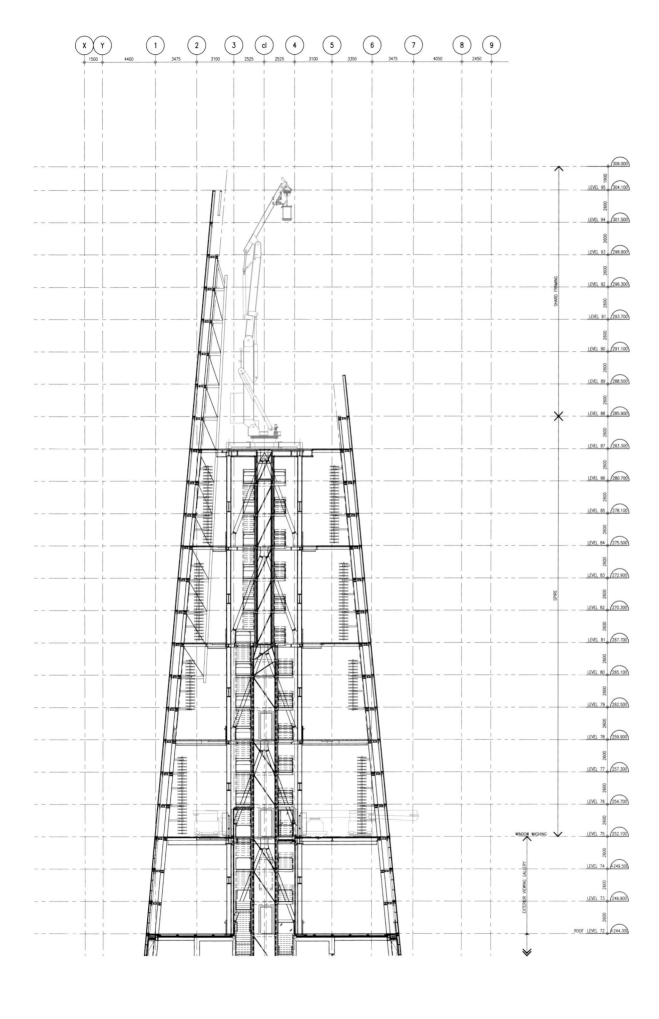

X Y 1 2 3 cl 4 5 6 7 8 9
1500 4400 3475 3100 2525 2525 3100 3350 3475 4050 2450

306.000
LEVEL 95 1900 304.100
LEVEL 94 2600 301.500
LEVEL 93 2600 298.900
LEVEL 92 2600 296.300
LEVEL 91 2600 293.700
LEVEL 90 2600 291.100
LEVEL 89 2600 288.500
LEVEL 88 2600 285.900
LEVEL 87 2600 283.300
LEVEL 86 2600 280.700
LEVEL 85 2600 278.100
LEVEL 84 2600 275.500
LEVEL 83 2600 272.900
LEVEL 82 2600 270.300
LEVEL 81 2600 267.700
LEVEL 80 2600 265.100
LEVEL 79 2600 262.500
LEVEL 78 2600 259.900
LEVEL 77 2600 257.300
LEVEL 76 2600 254.700
WINDOW WASHING LEVEL 75 2600 252.100
LEVEL 74 2600 249.500
LEVEL 73 2600 246.900
ROOF LEVEL 72 244.300

SHARD FRAMING
SPIRE
EXTERIOR VIEWING GALLERY

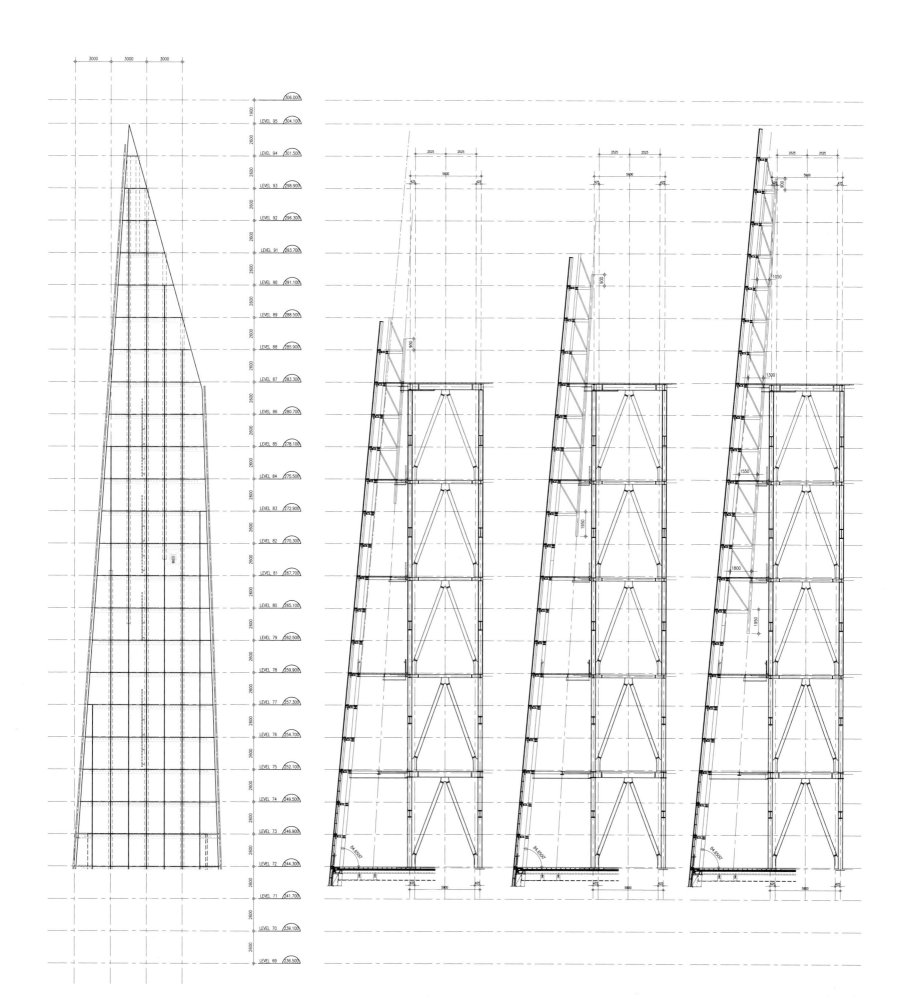

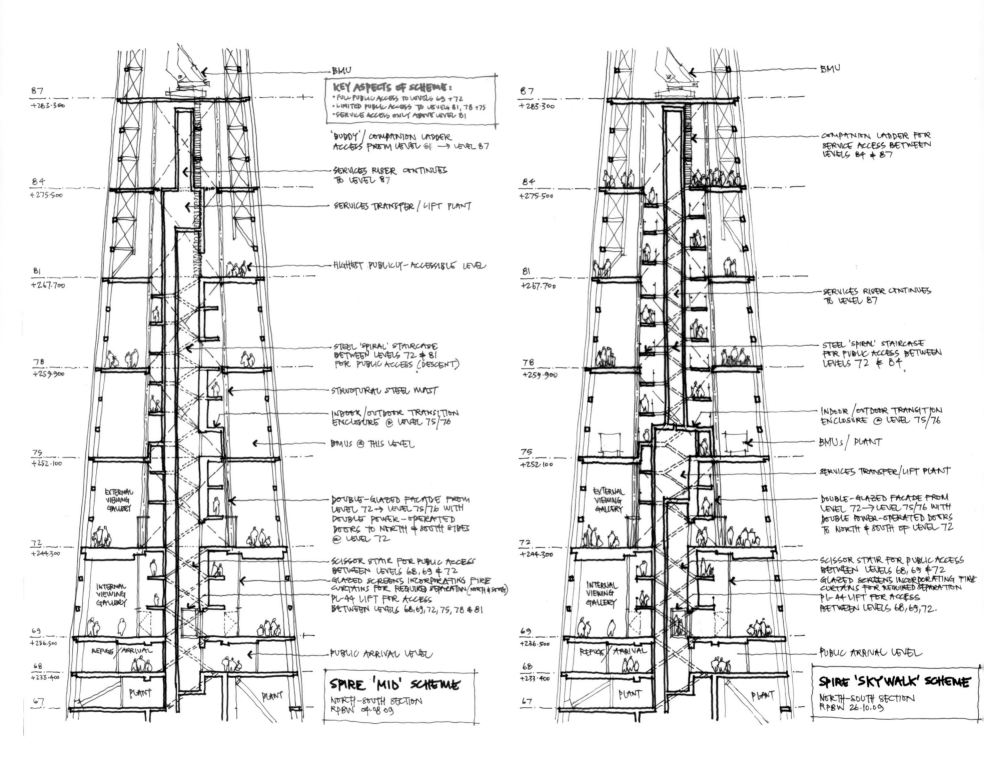

Left diagram:

87
+283.300

84
+275.500

81
+267.700

78
+259.900

75
+252.100

72
+244.300

69
+236.500

68
+233.400

67

EXTERNAL VIEWING GALLERY

INTERNAL VIEWING GALLERY

REFUGE / ARRIVAL

PLANT

PLANT

BMU

KEY ASPECTS OF SCHEME:
- FULL PUBLIC ACCESS TO LEVELS 69 +72
- LIMITED PUBLIC ACCESS TO LEVELS 81, 78 +75
- SERVICE ACCESS ONLY ABOVE LEVEL 81

'BUDDY' / COMPANION LADDER ACCESS FROM LEVEL 81 → LEVEL 87

SERVICES RISER CONTINUES TO LEVEL 87

SERVICES TRANSFER / LIFT PLANT

HIGHEST PUBLICLY-ACCESSIBLE LEVEL

STEEL 'SPIRAL' STAIRCASE BETWEEN LEVELS 72 & 81 FOR PUBLIC ACCESS (DESCENT)

STRUCTURAL STEEL MAST

INDOOR / OUTDOOR TRANSITION ENCLOSURE @ LEVEL 75/76

BMUS @ THIS LEVEL

DOUBLE-GLAZED FACADE FROM LEVEL 72 → LEVEL 75/76 WITH DOUBLE POWER-OPERATED DOORS TO NORTH & SOUTH SIDES @ LEVEL 72

SCISSOR STAIR FOR PUBLIC ACCESS BETWEEN LEVELS 68, 69 & 72 GLAZED SCREENS INCORPORATING FIRE CURTAINS FOR REQUIRED SEPARATION (NORTH & SOUTH) PL-44 LIFT FOR ACCESS BETWEEN LEVELS 68,69, 72, 75, 78 & 81

PUBLIC ARRIVAL LEVEL

SPIRE 'MID' SCHEME
NORTH-SOUTH SECTION
RPBW 04.08.09

Right diagram:

87
+283.300

84
+275.500

81
+267.700

78
+259.900

75
+252.100

72
+244.300

69
+236.500

68
+233.400

67

EXTERNAL VIEWING GALLERY

INTERNAL VIEWING GALLERY

REFUGE / ARRIVAL

PLANT

PLANT

BMU

COMPANION LADDER FOR SERVICE ACCESS BETWEEN LEVELS 84 & 87

SERVICES RISER CONTINUES TO LEVEL 87

STEEL 'SPIRAL' STAIRCASE FOR PUBLIC ACCESS BETWEEN LEVELS 72 & 84

INDOOR / OUTDOOR TRANSITION ENCLOSURE @ LEVEL 75/76

BMUS / PLANT

SERVICES TRANSFER / LIFT PLANT

DOUBLE-GLAZED FACADE FROM LEVEL 72 → LEVEL 75/76 WITH DOUBLE POWER-OPERATED DOORS TO NORTH & SOUTH OF LEVEL 72

SCISSOR STAIR FOR PUBLIC ACCESS BETWEEN LEVELS 68, 69 & 72 GLAZED SCREENS INCORPORATING FIRE CURTAINS FOR REQUIRED SEPARATION PL-44 LIFT FOR ACCESS BETWEEN LEVELS 68, 69, 72.

PUBLIC ARRIVAL LEVEL

SPIRE 'SKYWALK' SCHEME
NORTH-SOUTH SECTION
RPBW 26.10.09

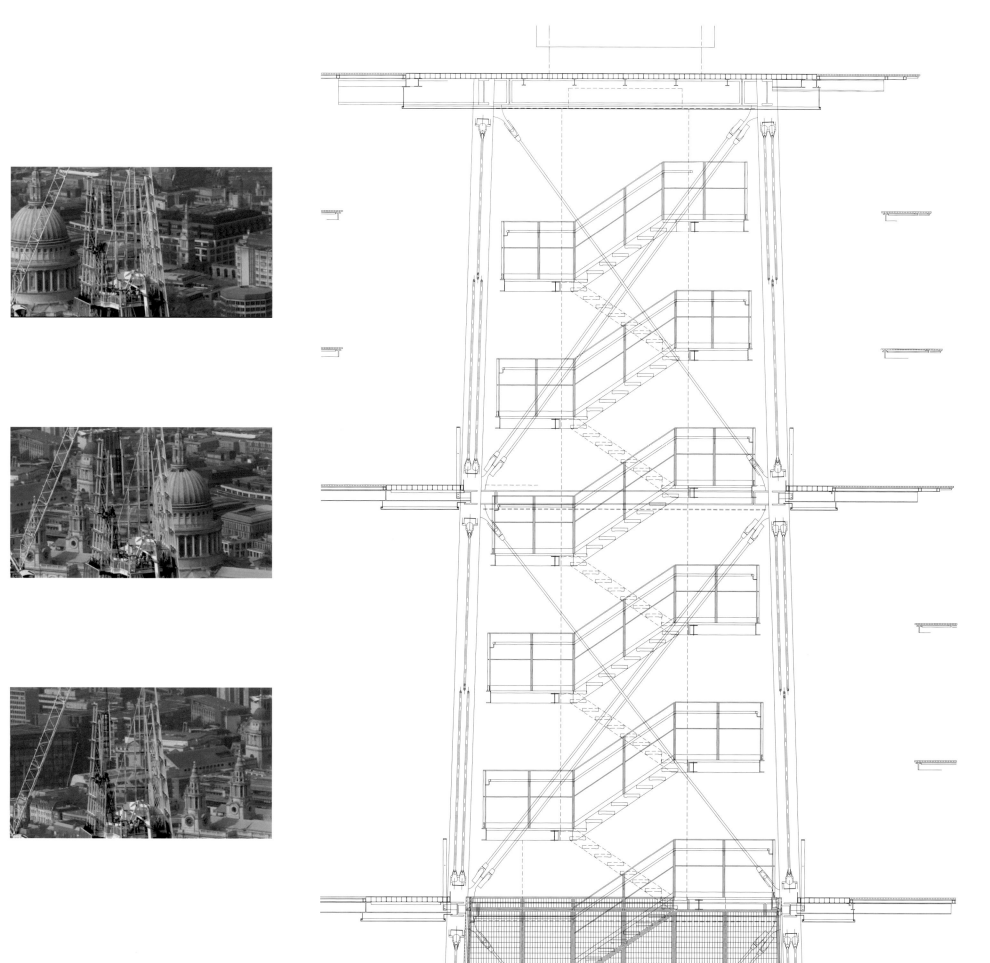

Le facciate quando arrivano alla sommità della torre non si chiudono, restano aperte, come se respirassero. In qualche maniera aspirano a un punto che però non raggiungono.

When the shards reach the top of the tower, they do not touch, but rather remain open as if they were to breathe. They seem to reach for a point that they are unable to achieve.

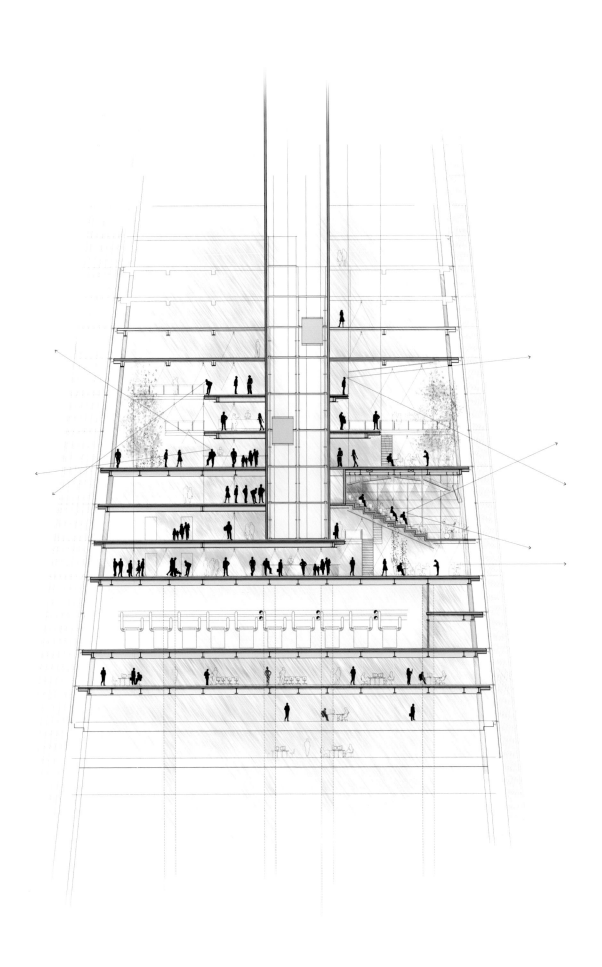

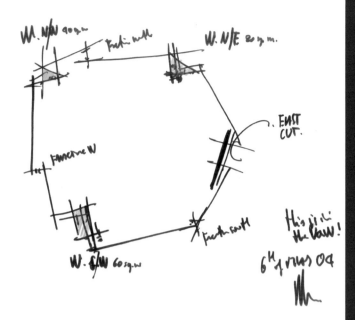

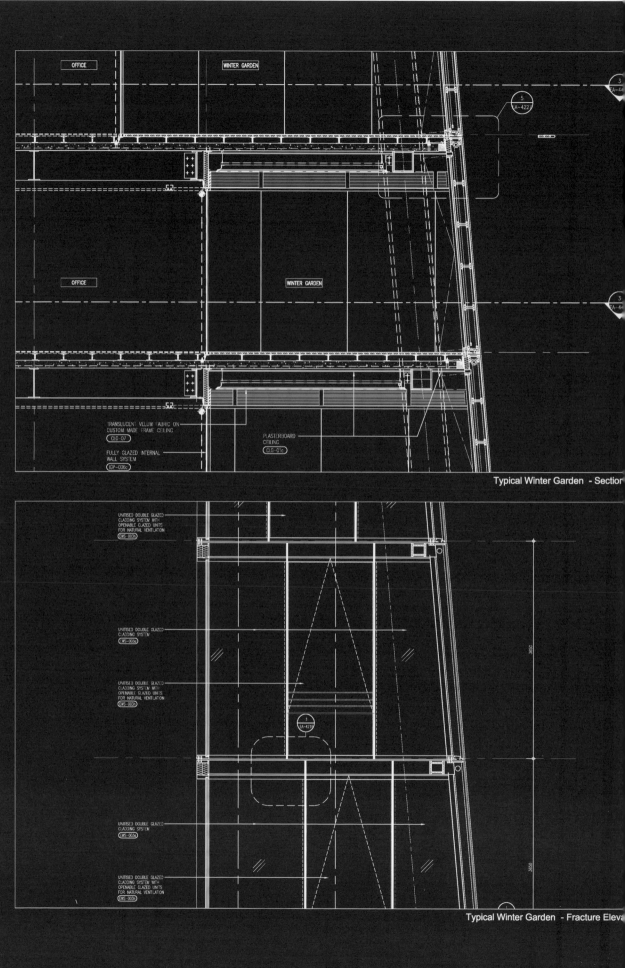

Typical Winter Garden - Section

Typical Winter Garden - Fracture Eleva

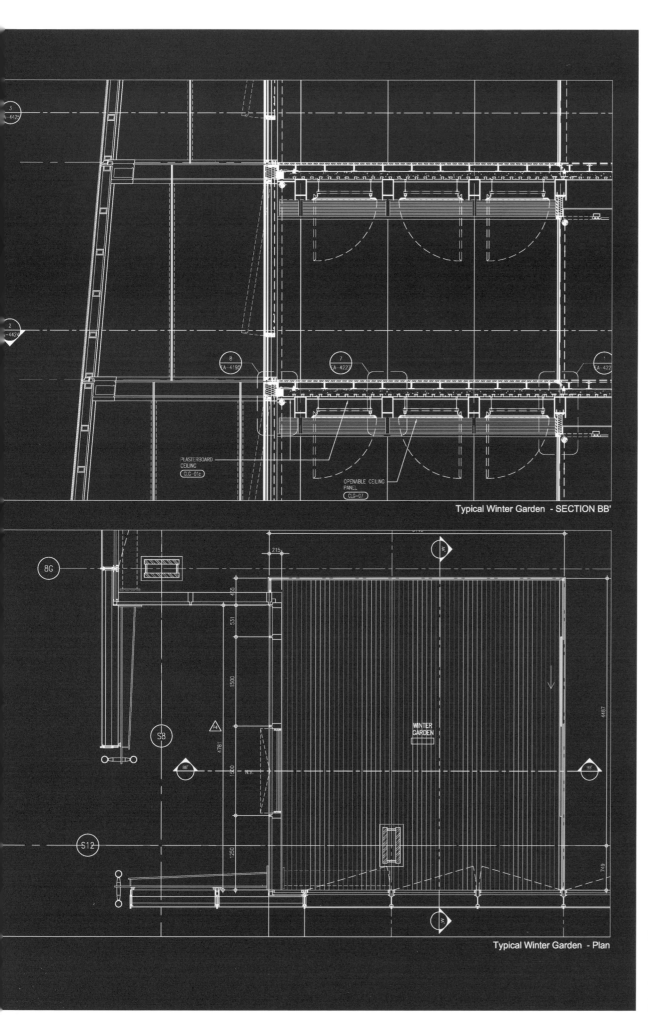

PLASTERBOARD
CEILING
CLG-01c

OPENABLE CEILING
PANEL
CLG-07

Typical Winter Garden - SECTION BB'

WINTER
GARDEN

Typical Winter Garden - Plan

Il metodo di costruzione cambia in relazione all'altezza dell'edificio. I piani interrati sono in cemento e ospitano i vani macchina, il parcheggio, l'hotel e le aree di servizio.
Il nucleo (the core), dal pian terreno fino al settantaduesimo piano, è in cemento armato vibrocompresso. I livelli inferiori e i piani ad uso ufficio hanno una struttura in acciaio, mentre i livelli residenziali e l'hotel impiegano solette in cemento post-compresso.
La guglia parte dal livello 75 e la struttura torna ad essere in acciaio. Il sistema di stabilità laterale si fonda su un nucleo verticale a mensola rinforzato con un sistema di travature di stabilizzazione (hat truss) ai livelli 66-67. Questo incrementa la rigidezza dell'edificio e riduce l'oscillazione generale della torre fino a +/- 500 mm in condizioni di forte vento.
Il basement è stato costruito con il sistema "top-down": le pareti sono alla berlinese, costituite da pali di diametro 900 mm e anima 700 mm. Il ricorso al sistema "top-down" non solo produce una struttura più efficiente, ma ha anche permesso di risparmiare tre mesi di lavoro rispetto al programma iniziale. La posizione centrale del nucleo permette l'ottimizzazione delle vie di fuga e della distribuzione dei servizi, mentre le pareti in cemento costituiscono un "cappotto" robusto e ignifugo.
La configurazione interna è dettata dalla necessità di ospitare la complessa strategia di trasporto verticale, indispensabile in un edificio a uso misto con diverse tipologie di affitto. In pianta, il nucleo è concepito come un insieme di vani rettangolari che assolvono a specifiche funzioni: come il vano ascensore, il corpo scale o un montacarichi di servizio. Lungo tutta l'altezza dell'edificio ognuno di questi vani può accogliere più di una funzione. Per esempio un vano ascensore ai livelli degli uffici può alloggiare un ascensore limitato a singoli piani o addirittura le scale nei piani residenziali. In tal modo viene ottimizzata l'efficienza degli spazi all'interno del nucleo.
Con l'aumentare dell'altezza si riducono i requisiti di stabilità laterale e i servizi, di conseguenza i vani del nucleo diminuiscono.
W.M.
.....

.....
The method of construction changes with the height of the building. The basement floors are in concrete and accommodate plant rooms, car parking, hotel and building service areas. The core is a slip formed concrete shaft, running from the basement to level 72. The lower levels and office floors are framed in steel and the residential and hotel levels use post-tensioned concrete floor slabs. At level 75 the spire begins and the structure reverts to steel. The lateral stability system is based on a vertical cantilevered core stiffened by an outrigger hat truss at levels 66-67. This enhancement to the stiffness of the building reduces the overall building sway in high wind conditions to +/- 500 mm.
The multi-level basement was constructed using top-down construction methods.
The basement wall is a secant pile wall, comprising of 900 mm diameter piles at 700 mm centres. The use of top-down construction not only produces a more efficient structure, but also saved 3 months on the construction programme.
Positioned centrally within the floor plate, the core allows for the optimization of escape distances and servicing distribution while the concrete walls provide a robust and fire-resistant enclosure. The internal configuration is dictated by the need to accommodate the complex vertical transportation strategy necessary to service a multi-tenanted mixed use building. On plan, the core is conceived as a collection of rectangular boxes/shafts that contain a specific function such as a lift shaft, stairwell or service riser.
Over the height of the building a particular riser may accommodate more than one function. For example, a lift shaft in the office levels may house a different local lift or even a stairwell in the residential floors. In this way the efficiency of space within the core is optimised. With increasing height, elements/boxes terminate with the reduction of servicing and lateral stability requirements and the core reduces in size.
W.M.
.....

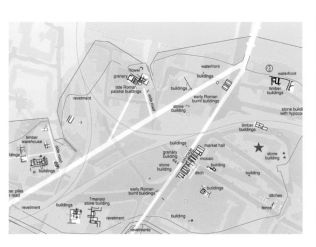

Durante gli scavi ci sono stati due ritrovamenti archeologici: il primo nel 2011, una villa romana del II sec. A.C., e il secondo pochi giorni fa, sul cantiere della London Bridge House, un edificio per uffici che sta nascendo di fronte allo Shard.

We unearthed two significant archaeological finds during the site preparations: the first, in 2011, was a Roman villa from the second century B.C. The second was discovered more recently on the site of London Bridge House, where an office building, also part of the scheme, is being erected opposite the Shard.

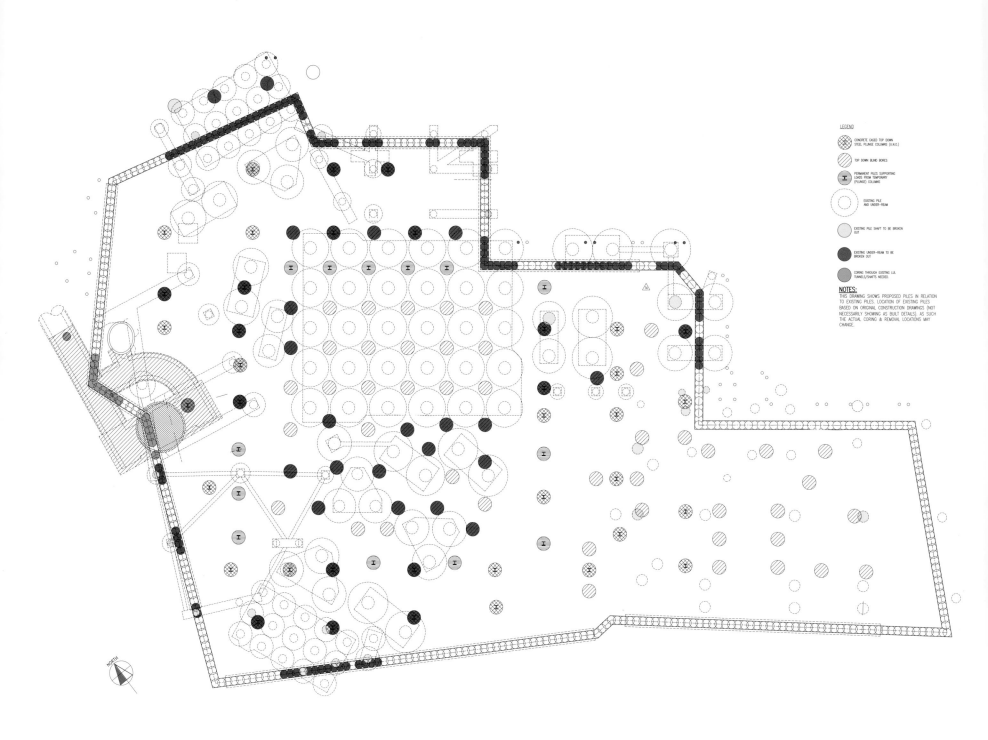

LEGEND

CONCRETE CASED TOP DOWN STEEL PLUNGE COLUMNS (U.N.O.)

TOP DOWN BLIND BORES

PERMANENT PILES SUPPORTING LOADS FROM TEMPORARY (PLUNGE) COLUMNS

EXISTING PILE AND UNDER-REAM

EXISTING PILE SHAFT TO BE BROKEN OUT

EXISTING UNDER-REAM TO BE BROKEN OUT

CORING THROUGH EXISTING L.U.L. TUNNELS/SHAFTS NEEDED

NOTES:
THIS DRAWING SHOWS PROPOSED PILES IN RELATION TO EXISTING PILES. LOCATION OF EXISTING PILES BASED ON ORIGINAL CONSTRUCTION DRAWINGS (NOT NECESSARILY SHOWING AS BUILT DETAILS). AS SUCH THE ACTUAL CORING & REMOVAL LOCATIONS MAY CHANGE.

NORTH

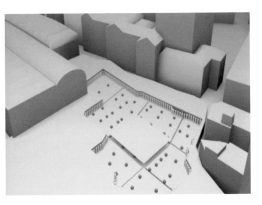

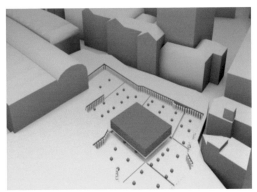

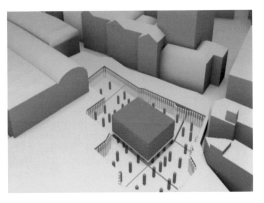

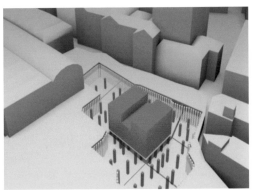

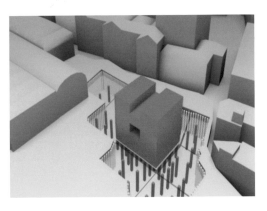

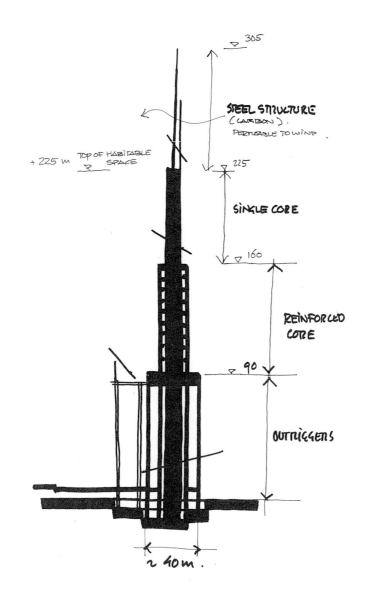

305

STEEL STRUCTURE
(CARBON).
PERMEABLE TO WIND.

+ 225 m   TOP OF HABITABLE
              SPACE

225

SINGLE CORE

160

REINFORCED
CORE

90

OUTRIGGERS

~ 40 m.

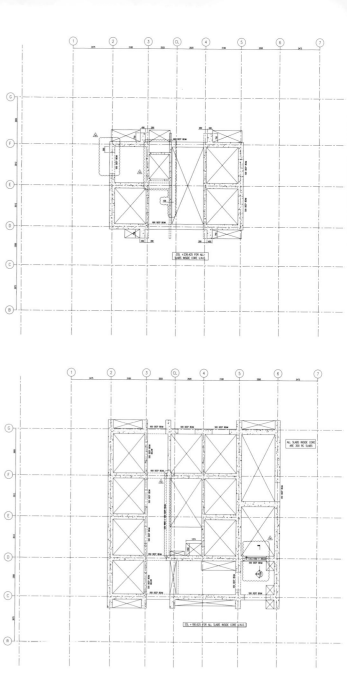

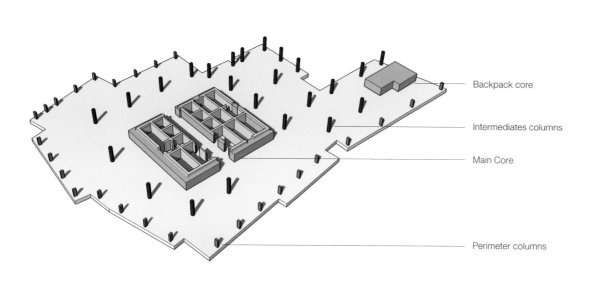

Backpack core

Intermediates columns

Main Core

Perimeter columns

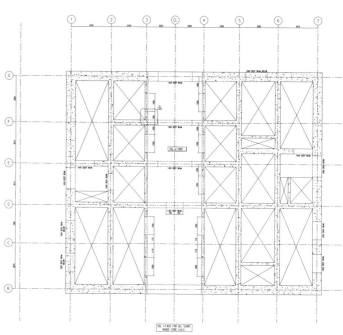

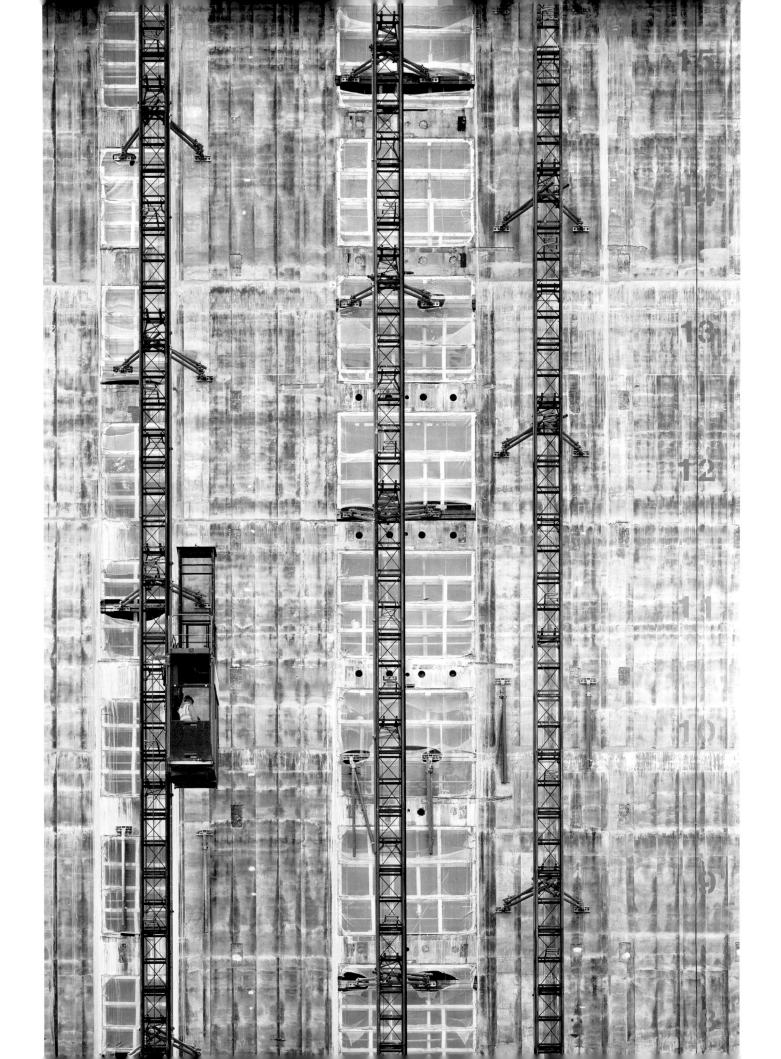

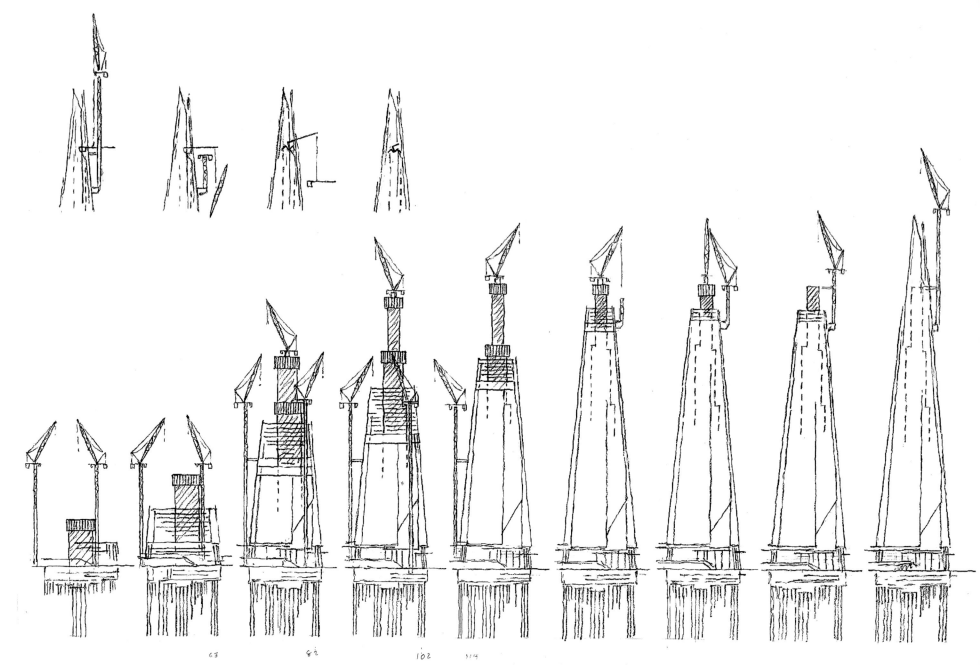

63   82   102   124

In cantiere ha lavorato una squadra
di alpinisti. I pezzi erano montati a 300 metri
di altezza, con il vento che può arrivare
a 80 chilometri all'ora.

A team of climbers was employed at the site.
The parts were assembled 300 meters
above the ground, with gusts of wind reaching
80 km/h.

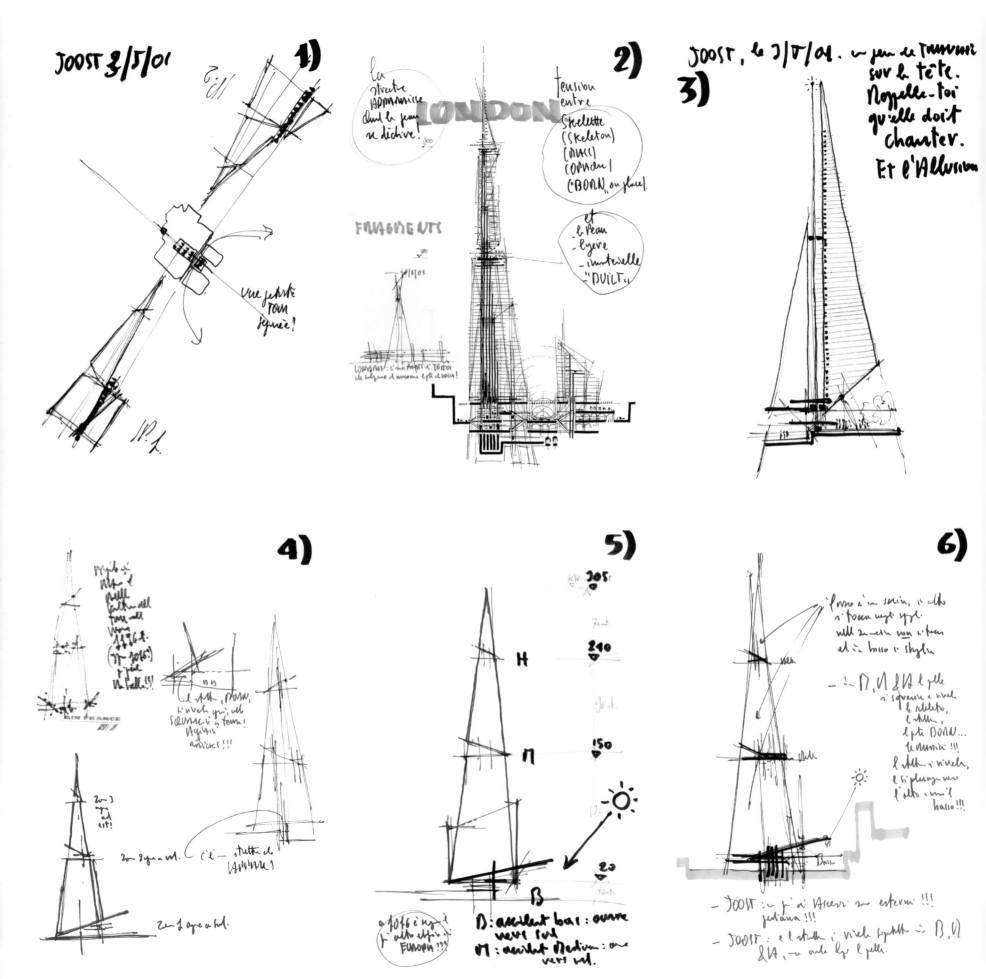

114

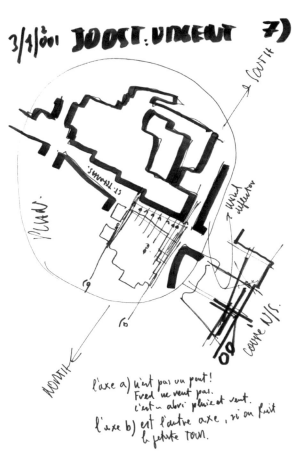

© Rob Telford.
www.Cybertects.co.uk

3/4/01 **JOOST. VINCENT 7)**

l'axe a) n'est pas un pont!
Fred ne veut pas.
c'est un abri pluie et vent.
l'axe b) est l'autre axe, si on fait
la petite tour.

Un cantiere avventuroso: hanno persino catturato una volpe che viveva da settimane a 280 metri di altezza, rubando i pranzi agli operai.

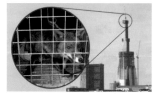

An adventurous site: they even caught a fox that had been living almost 280 meters above the ground for weeks, stealing the workers' lunches.

La sera dell'inaugurazione, nel luglio del 2012, Irvine Sellar aveva organizzato una cena al Billingsgate Market dall'altra parte del fiume, accompagnata da uno show di laser. Dopo l'evento siamo tornati a piedi attraversando il London Bridge.

Con nostra sorpresa e grande stupore, il ponte era chiuso al traffico, perché 100.000 londinesi si erano riversati lì per ammirare l'evento e si erano fermati, godendosi la serata estiva, per continuare a guardare l'edificio. Non lo dimenticheremo mai.

The evening of the 'opening' ceremony, in July 2012, Irvine Sellar organised a dinner at Billingsgate just across the river, accompanied by a laser show on the Shard. After the event we strolled back over London Bridge. To our surprise and stupefaction the bridge was unexpectedly closed to traffic because 300,000 Londoners had come down spontaneously to watch the event of the Shard and had stayed on to enjoy in company the summer evening while still viewing the building. We will never forget that.

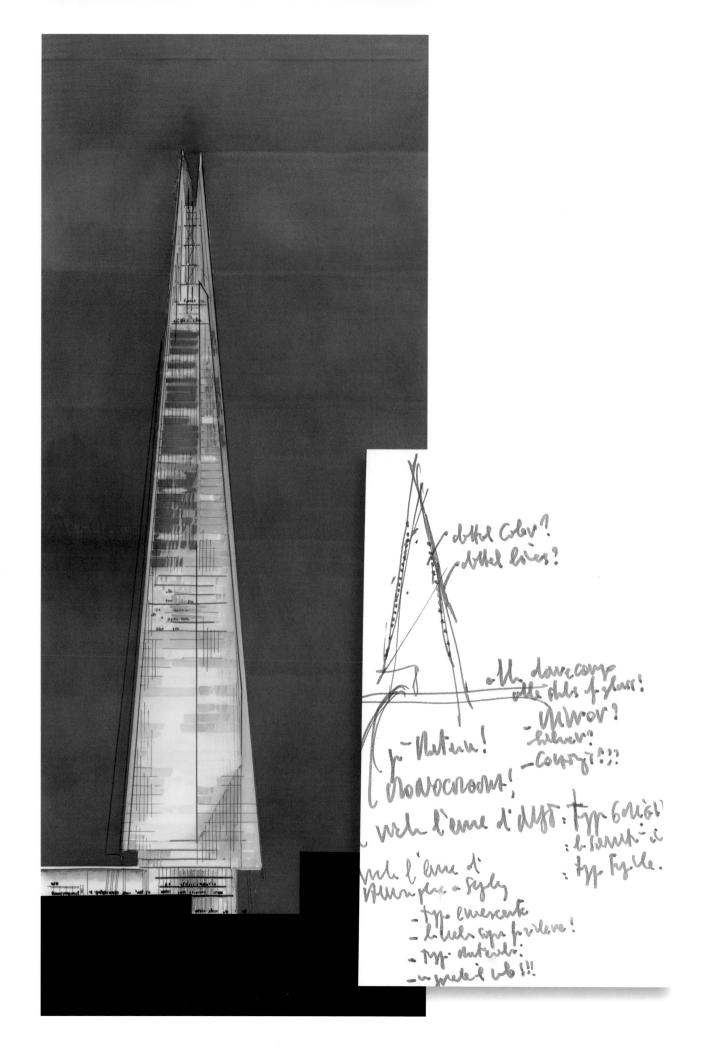

ST. THOMAS Street.

LONDON

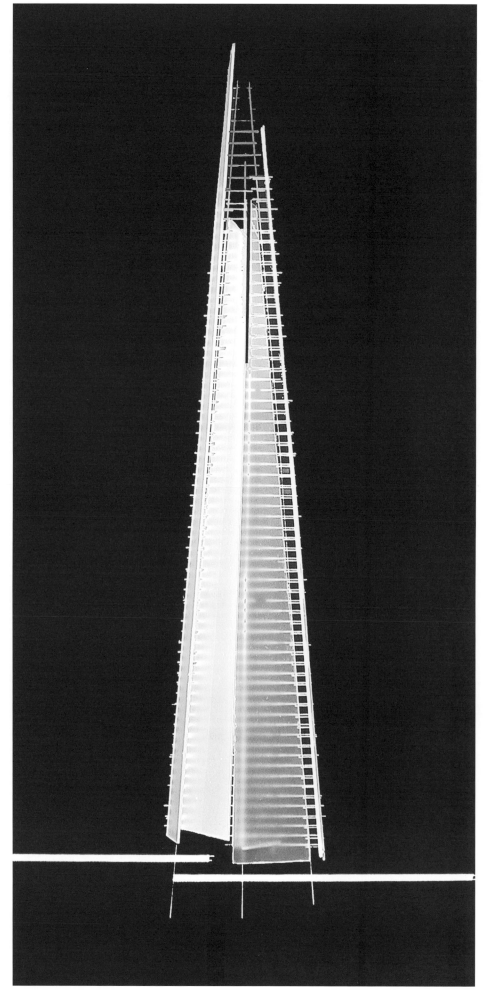

Renzo Piano, Joost Moolhuijzen, Irvine Sellar,
William Matthews.

Renzo Piano, Richard and Ruth Rogers

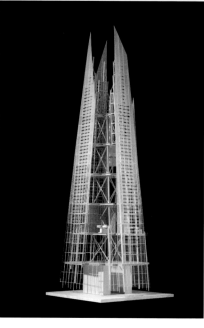

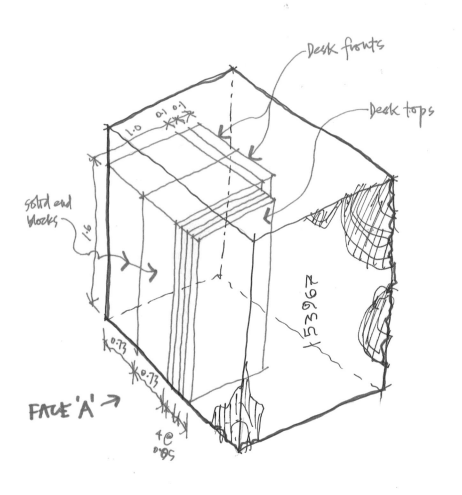

Desk fronts

Desk tops

solid end blocks

1.0   0.1 0.1

1.6

53967

0.73
0.73
4 @ 0.85

FACE 'A' →

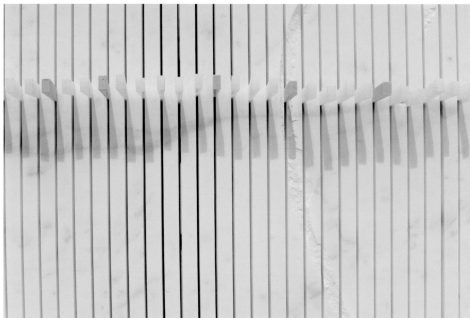

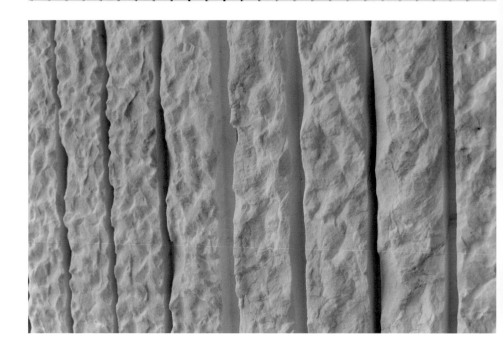

SHARD OFFICE LOBBY RECEPTION DESK
MARBLE BLOCK CUTTING PROPOSAL

RPBW 20.12.11

.....
Il nucleo centrale è rivestito in marmo Calacatta Apuano originario della zona di Carrara, in Italia.
I blocchi di marmo sono stati tagliati a "fette", quindi cesellati a mano per evidenziare la profondità e il carattere del materiale. Il rivestimento esterno in pietra può a volte apparire sottile, quasi con un effetto carta da parati. Trattando in questo modo il materiale, miravamo a riflettere la solidità del nucleo stesso.
W.M.
.....

.....
The central core is clad in Calacatta Apuano marble from the Carrara region of Italy. The blocks of marble were sliced into slabs and then hand chiseled to show the depth and character of the material. Stone cladding can sometimes appear like a thin veneer applied as wallpaper. By expressing the material we aimed to reflect the solidity of the core itself.
W.M.
.....

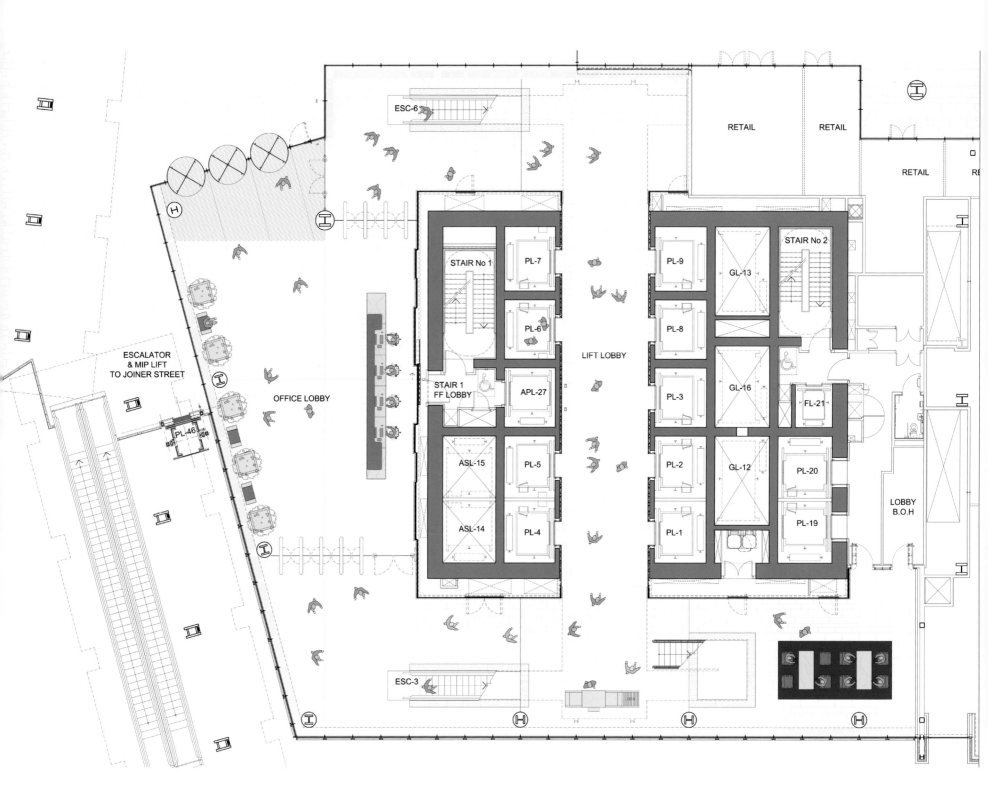

ESC-6

RETAIL   RETAIL

RETAIL

STAIR No 1   PL-7

STAIR No 2

PL-9   GL-13

PL-6

PL-8

LIFT LOBBY

ESCALATOR
& MIP LIFT
TO JOINER STREET

OFFICE LOBBY

STAIR 1
FF LOBBY   APL-27

PL-3   GL-16

FL-21

PL-46

ASL-15   PL-5

PL-2   GL-12   PL-20

LOBBY
B.O.H

ASL-14   PL-4

PL-1   PL-19

ESC-3

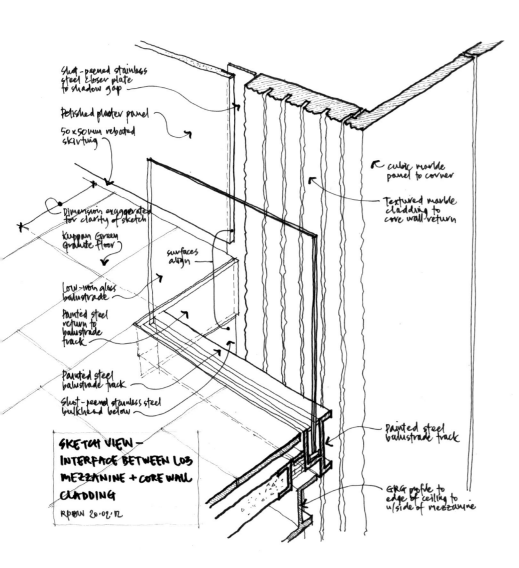

shot-peened stainless steel closer plate to shadow gap

Polished plaster panel

50 x 50mm rebated skirting

Dimension exaggerated for clarity of sketch

Kuppam Green Granite floor

Low-iron glass balustrade

Painted steel return to balustrade track

Painted steel balustrade track

Shot-peened stainless steel bulkhead below

cubic marble panel to corner

Textured marble cladding to core wall return

surfaces align

Painted steel balustrade track

GRG profile to edge of ceiling to u/side of mezzanine

SKETCH VIEW –
INTERFACE BETWEEN L03
MEZZANINE + CORE WALL
CLADDING

RPBW 20.02.12

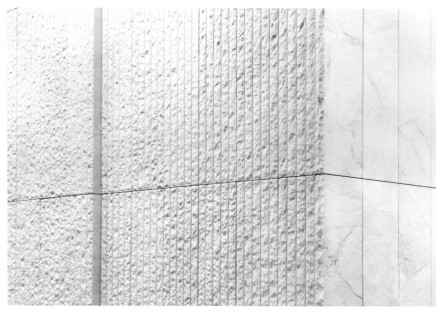

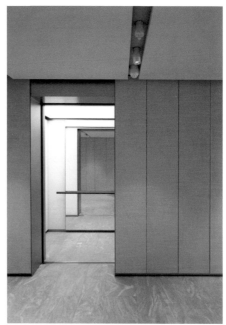

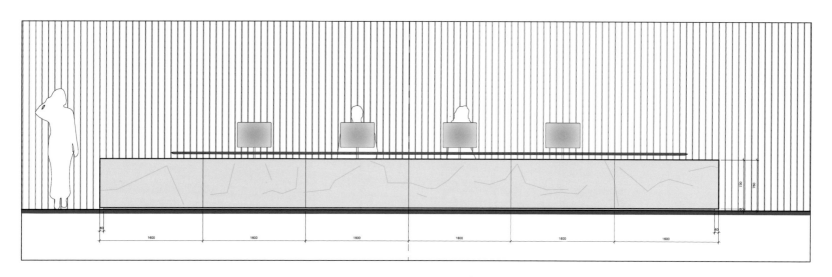

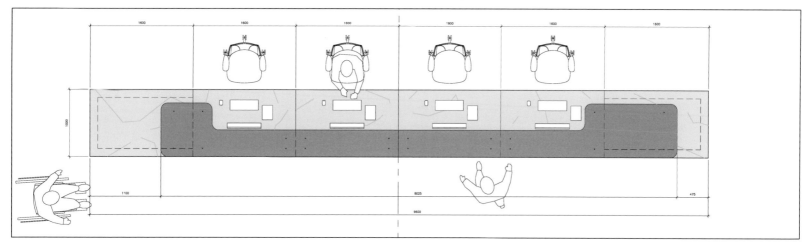

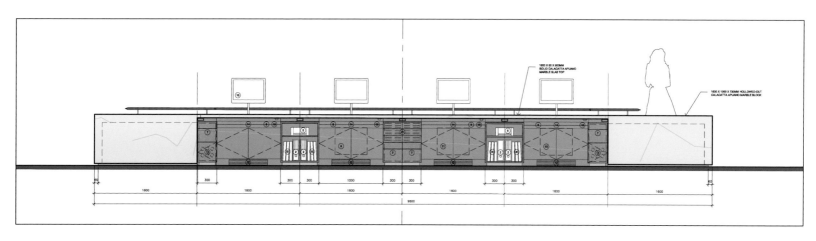

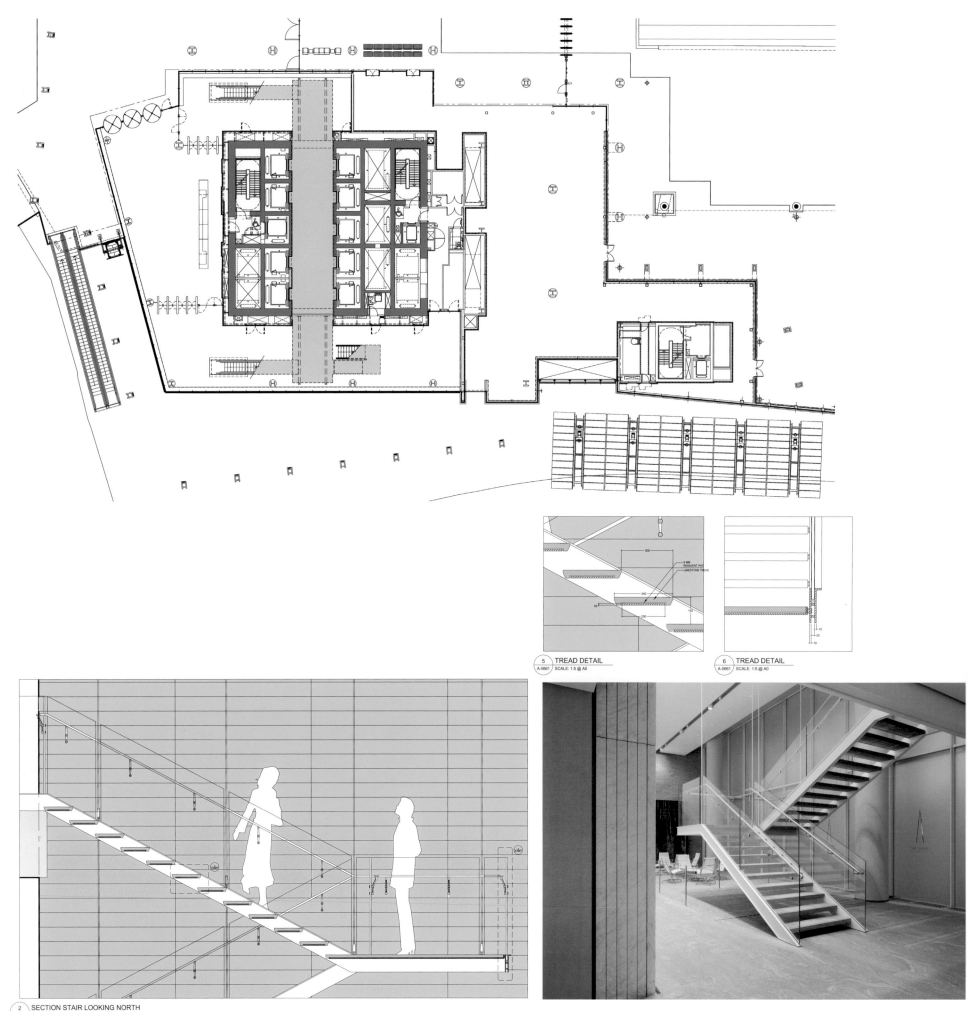

5   TREAD DETAIL
A-5661   SCALE: 1:5 @ A0

6   TREAD DETAIL
A-5661   SCALE: 1:5 @ A0

2   SECTION STAIR LOOKING NORTH
A-5661   SCALE: 1:10 @ A0

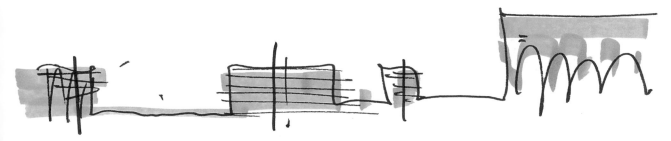

Era importante che la torre, nonostante fluttuasse sopra la città, fosse saldamente radicata al suo *topos*. La Stazione di London Bridge e i viadotti ferroviari verso est e ovest sono caratterizzati dall'uso del mattone, e sembrava appropriato fare ricorso allo stesso materiale per la base della torre. I mattoni sono stati prodotti a mano nello Yorkshire utilizzando un'argilla simile per colore e consistenza a quella usata in origine a Londra.
W. M.

It was important that the Tower, floating above the city, was also rooted in it's *topos*. London Bridge Station and the railway viaducts to the east and west are entirely based upon brick structures and it seemed appropriate to use the same material for the foot of the tower. The bricks were handmade in Yorkshire using a clay similar in colour and texture to original London stock.
W. M.

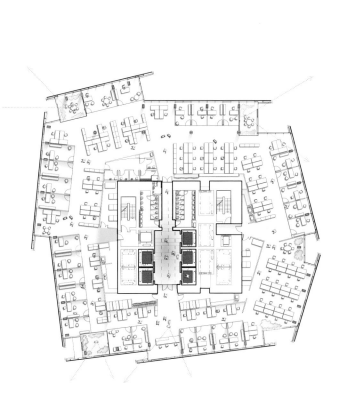

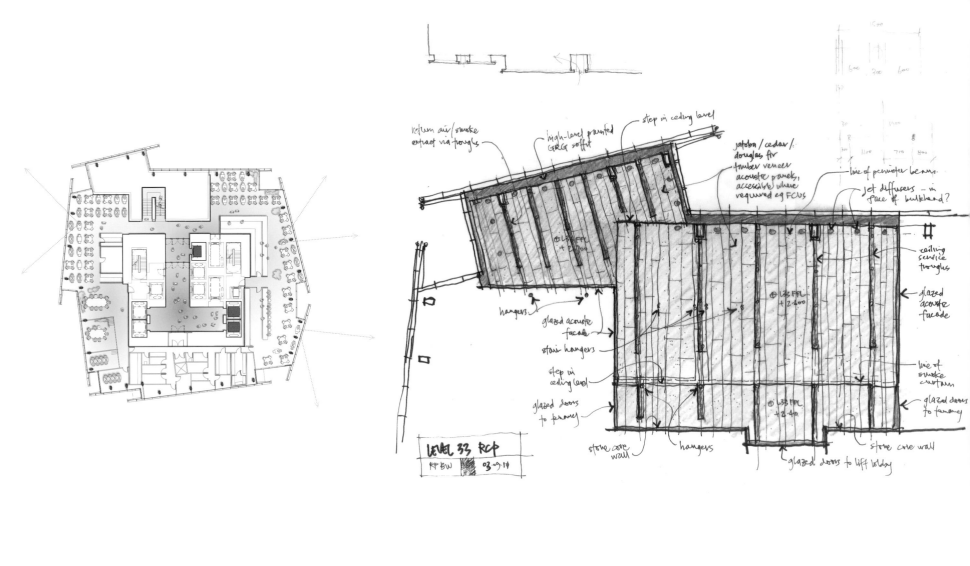

return air/smoke
extract via troughs

high-level painted
GRG/G soffit

step in ceiling level

jatoba / cedar /
douglas fir
timber veneer
acoustic panels,
accessible where
required eg FCUs

line of perimeter beams.

jet diffusers – in
face of bulkhead?

ceiling service
troughs

glazed
acoustic
facade

hangers

glazed acoustic
facade

stair hangers

step in
ceiling level

glazed doors
to balcony

line of
smoke
curtain

glazed doors
to balcony

stone core
wall

hangers

stone core wall

glazed doors to lift lobby

LEVEL 33 RCP
RPBW   03-09-14

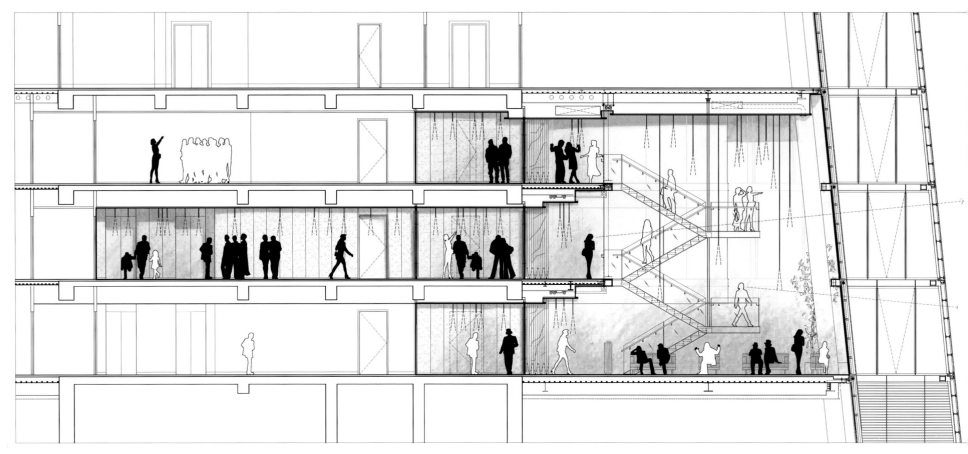

A St Paul's for our time

Norman Rosenthal

Who cares who built it or why? The Shard is simply London's finest building since Wren's masterpiece

The reactions to London's latest mega-structure have not been moderate. "The Shard has slashed the face of London forever," wrote Simon Jenkins in the Guardian a month ago, invoking the destruction of Timbuktu, Dresden, Moscow and Peking. Jonathan Jones, the Guardian's art critic, has described the Shard as "self-evidently a monument to wealth and power run way out of control. It screams with dazzling arrogance that money rules this city and says money inhabits a realm way above our heads."

But when have great buildings and structures - since the pyramids of Egypt and before - been anything other than monuments to wealth and power? The fact is that, in recent decades, power has resulted in many vulgar blots on the landscape. London, of course, was terribly damaged during the second world war. Bomb sites scarred the city and, for the most part, what has come to replace them has been pretty abominable architecturally, with only a few exceptions. Any sensitive person crossing the Thames on Norman Foster's pedestrian bridge, looking left and right towards Christopher Wren's Baroque masterpiece, can only want to put on blinkers. Nasty skyscrapers have been built all over the West End and the City of London, from Centrepoint to the former NatWest Tower, not to mention London's Barbican. Here, many wonderful cultural events take place, but it can only be described as a planning monstrosity.

Finally, along comes something that is genuinely magnificent to look at - namely the Shard, as it has affectionately come to be known. I don't care about its function or who built it, or even who financed it. It is a masterpiece of visual design by one of the great living architects, Renzo Piano.

Its apparently broken apex makes for one astonishingly poetic image. As a pure glass edifice it resembles the most amazing cut diamond, both by day in the sunshine and at night lit up as a beacon over the city, as thrilling as the Eiffel Tower in Paris – which was also hated by establishment figures when it first went up. Now we cannot imagine Paris without it. I cannot now imagine London without the Shard and would go so far as to say that it is arguably the greatest and most beautifully skyreaching building to be erected in London since St Paul's Cathedral.

Critics who profess to be concerned with London and the way it looks would spend their energy better if they were to turn their attention to those ghastly sculptures mushrooming up all over the city's squares and parks. The idea of walking around Hyde Park and Kensington Gardens now fills me with horror as my eyes are continually assaulted by absurd and corrupt objects such as the horse's head at Marble Arch, not to mention the stupid jelly babies nearby, or the monument to the poor animals killed in the two world wars.

The beautiful Royal Artillery Memorial has been horribly upstaged by a succession of hideous monuments commemorating fallen heroes of the Commonwealth, most recently a ghastly parody of the beautiful screen of Decimus Burton next to Apsley House. One can argue about the rights and wrongs of erecting a monument to Bomber Harris, who in the understandable hysteria of the second world war caused, among other things, the destruction of the beautiful city of Dresden. What one can also argue, if one has any aesthetic sensibility, is that the retrograde and cheap monument is the most ghastly eyesore and should have been prevented.

In the meantime, one can only be grateful that at least the Shard is here to give continual visual pleasure from all aspects and distances across town. Don't you love the story of the fox that climbed to its top? How happy it must have been!

Norman Rosenthal is former head of exhibitions at the Royal Academy

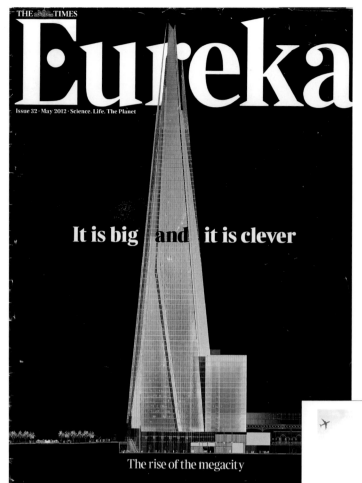

THE TIMES

Eureka

Issue 32 · May 2012 · Science. Life. The Planet

It is big and it is clever

The rise of the megacity

HIGH & MIGHTY

Tall buildings got off to a poor start with the Tower of Babel, but the sky really is no limit now

Words: Michael Hanlon
Model maker: Hattie Newman
Illustration: Sam Green

SKYSCRAPERS

---

country's energy bill and reducing our dependence on supplies from countries such as Russia. Even so, it is likely that British gas prices will fall

ing in Britain is not nearly as low as that in the US.

but in the long-term ... ain cannot afford

Big, Glassy and Beautiful

The Shard is a welcome addition to the skyline of Lon

boozled traditionally spire-loving clergymen by suggesting he had abandoned plans for a huge dome, only to horrify them with a mammarian fait accompli. The Millennium Dome was taken to be a metaphor for spiritual emptiness by critics, and is now an indispensable London landmark. It is not all unlikely that the completion of the White Tower, London's tallest building till 1310, was greeted with derision by Thameside lovers of wattle and daub. Heritage campaigners are part of a long and melancholy tradition of architectural conservatism in their dislike of the Shard.

Architects are true that there a buildings in Lon hideous — the c — is now offset b

But the United has constantly ch to commerce an scape has chang Shard does not and confident, it thrust above the

Opinion and weather 17 **Letters** 20 **World** 23 **Features** 40 **Busin**

The Shard has slashed the face of London for ever

Simon Jenkins

Timbuktu's shrines can be rebuilt but this tower, and the glass forest that's set to follow, will ruin the skyline of the capital

We are shocked by the news from Timbuktu. The Islamists are at it again, smashing the medieval shrines and mosques of the desert city, as they did the buddhas of Afghanistan. They claim these jewels of African heritage offend sharia law. Unesco calls the destruction "a tragedy for all humanity", and a prosecutor at the international criminal court calls it a war crime.

Perhaps they are right. As with the RAF bombing of Dresden, Stalin's dynamiting of Moscow churches and the bulldozing of old Peking, the wilful destruction of beauty in the name of progress offends civilised sensibility.

So what of tomorrow's bombastic celebration of the Shard's arrival on the London skyline? It too has drawn Unesco's ire for intruding on the Tower of London and Parliament Square. It will boost its hugeness with lights and lasers, and publicists will dismiss its critics as fuddy-duddies and aesthetes, proclaiming Shards for all time as angels of growth.

I suffer from having toured London's skyline a thing of beauty. The views from Parliament and Primrose hills, from the parks and from bridges over the Thames offered a vista that allowed the eye to spread, with no part dominating the whole. Even St Paul's did not crush its neighbours but floated above them at just twice their height.

The eye has no such freedom now. From across the London basin it must rest on the Shard. Its architect, Renzo Piano, claims that his creation "is not about arrogance and power" but intended "to celebrate community ... surprise and joy". Besides, it is so high "it will disappear into the sky". Architects have never been happy bedfellows with the English language. As for the tower's developer, Irvine Sellar, he suggests that his building is indeed about arrogance and power. He wants it to cry, "This is London, this is the Shard." Now, he says, "we can kick sand in the face of the Eiffel Tower."

This egomaniacal architecture echoes the tower's political backers, Ken Livingstone, John Prescott and Boris Johnson, who equate phallic prominence with civic prowess. They are in thrall to the Shard's Qatari financiers, who are said to see it as "non-pecuniary soft diplomacy". One Gulf expert explained that "if someone invades a country that has the highest skyscraper in town, then surely the UK should come to the rescue". The Shard is thus an adjunct of Tony Blair's foreign policy, a cure for erectile dysfunction.

This tower is anarchy. It conforms to no planning policy. It marks no architectural focus or rond-point. It offers no civic forum or function, just luxury flats and hotels. It stands apart from the City cluster and pays no heed to its surrounding context in scale, materials or ground presence. It seems to have lost its way from Dubai to Canary Wharf.

The Shard was furiously opposed by local people, by Southwark council and by historic buildings and conservation authorities. It was pushed as a symbol of Britain's love affair with financial bling at the turn of the 21st century, with "iconic" celebrities and the off-you greed of arbitrage. It was allowed to go ahead by Yorkshire's John Prescott as a single-finger gesture in the face of wimpish southerners.

There is no case for buildings like this on grounds of urban density. Their space ratios make them costly and inefficient to service. Any Londoner knows there are thousands of acres of unused and underused land within the M25 awaiting the high-density, low-rise building preferred by the property market.

Some people find the Shard beautiful. I am sure I would in the Gulf, as I admire the Burj Khalifa tower. But Bermondsey is not Dubai. Nor is this just a matter of one person's opinion against another's. It is the destruction of one for the other's gain. There are plenty of places for Sellar and Piano to play their games. Why must they tip paint over my Canaletto?

The Shard shows money trumping planning. Let one rise high and there is no case against another. The argument that London's skyline should be an open

market failed in its attempt to build over Hampstead Heath in the 19th century and to demolish Piccadilly Circus and much of Whitehall in the 20th. But it took courageous fighting against precisely the arguments deployed by the Shard's apologists.

Would they or their imitators now demand the right to build a shard on Blackheath, in Kensington Square – not, why not? Is it that the locals there are rich, whereas in Southwark they were poor? Or do we agree that there is something called beauty in townscape, but that Sellar and Piano claim the right to determine it for themselves.

The truth is that we have lost the ability to articulate what is beautiful for purposes of development control. We the small man cannot touch a door frame, the big one can do what he lik The clutch of permits awarded by Pre cott and Livingstone is about to yield a forest of towers behind the National Theatre, behind the Festival Hall, ove Waterloo station and at Vauxhall, where a tower is already looming over Pimli The precedent is set.

The Thames is to become a ditch cash running through a canyon of gl San Gimignano re-engineered as Bla Runner. This is planning in the age of Barclays, an oligarchy of wealth, a fin cial fanaticism every bit as selfish an destructive as the religious fanaticism of Timbuktu. But there is a difference Timbuktu's shrines can and surely w be rebuilt. The Shard has slashed the face of London for ever.

simon_jenkins@guardian.co.uk

> **Some find it beautiful. I'm sure I would in the Gulf, as I admire the Burj Khalifa. But Bermondsey is not Dubai**

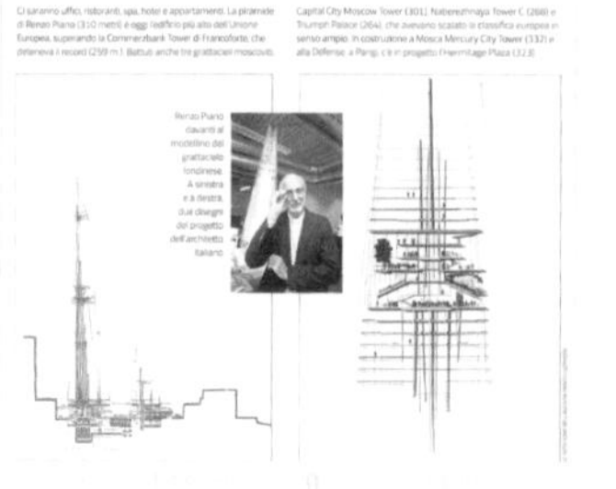

Comment & Debate

30

---

into care, it has a duty to provide better protection

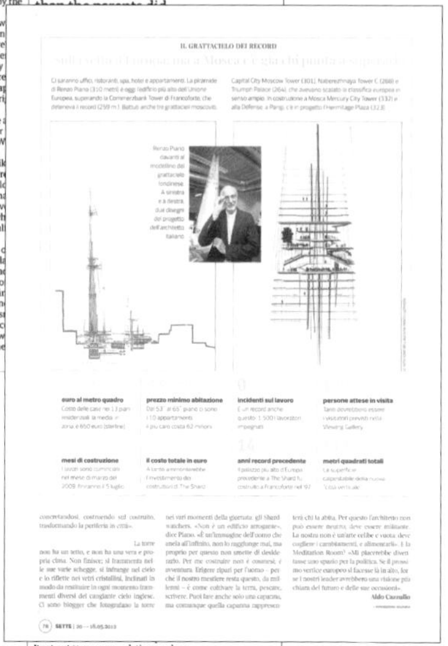

TRE per TE

Il Sole 24 O

www.ilsole24o...

QUOTIDIANO POLITICO ECONOMICO FIN

€ 2* In Italia obbligatorio con Racconti d'Autore. ... Domenica 24 Giugno 2012

LONDRA

La Scheggia più alta d'Europa

VERSO IL CIELO Il grattacielo costruito ... londinese di St. Giles

Lo Shard, il grattacielo di 306 metri realizzato da Renzo Piano, verrà inaugurato il 4 luglio. Ottantasette piani con abitazioni, hotel, uffici e una spettacolare «camera con vista» in cima

di Fulvio Irace

Un secolo e mezzo dopo il Crystal Palace, Londra avrà la piramide di cristallo. Più che una piramide, in realtà, una scheggia di cristallo, alta 306 metri (con 87 piani: la torre più alta d'Europa e certamente la più importante e (forse anche) più importante e (forse anche ingombrante).

Il Shard - la scheggia - è stata battezzata così da Renzo Piano, l'architetto italiano che ha strappato il primato nel campo del grattacieli in cui gli inglesi (con sir Norman Foster in testa) hanno sempre avuto una posizione di ribalta, sia per l'arditezza tecnologica che per l'innovazione tipologica e formale.

Chi si aspettava da Renzo Piano una performance simile al grattacielo del «New York Times» a Londra, nell'area centrale (ma derelitta) di St. Giles.

Eiffel Tower
Garnier
France 1889

For every doubling of housing density, car use drops by nearly 7 per cent

The Shard
Renzo Piano
London, UK 2012

The UK's new highest building is a good example of how years of innovative engineering have made skyscrapers possible

STRUCTURE · WALLS · SWAY · WIND

1,223 The number of skyscrapers in Hong Kong, the record holder

Cité Radieuse
Le Corbusier
Marseille, France 1947

£1.11bn The total cost of Taipei 101, the world's most expensive building

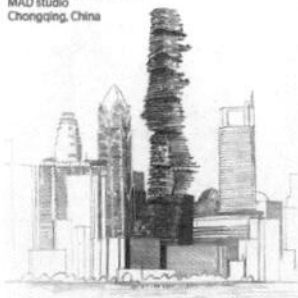
Urban Forest (proposed)
MAD studio
Chongqing, China

Sceptics claim that supertall buildings are simply ego-trips — phallic symbols

1007m The height of the Kingdom Tower in Jeddah, due to be completed in 2017

LIFTS
FOUNDATIONS
TRANSPORT
EARTHQUAKES
310 Metres
72 floors

The world's tallest buildings

BURJ KHALIFA
Dubai
828m
MAKKAH CLOCK ROYAL TOWER
Makkah, Saudi Arabia
601m
TAIPEI 101
Taipei
509m
SHANGHAI WORLD FINANCIAL CENTRE
Shanghai
492m
INTERNATIONAL COMMERCE CENTRE
Hong Kong
484m

43.34 Number of football pitches that will fit in the 305,000m² Burj Khalifa, Dubai

Le Monde
Samedi 7 juillet 2012

The Telegraph

HOME | NEWS | WORLD | SPORT | FINANCE | COMMENT | BLOGS | CULTURE | TRAVEL | LIFE | FA

Politics | Obits | Education | Earth | Science | Defence | Health | Scotland | Royal | Celebriti

HOME » NEWS » NEWS TOPICS » HOW ABOUT THAT?

Fox found living at top of Europe's tallest skyscraper

An inquisitive fox has been found living at the top of the Shard in London, Europe's tallest skyscraper.

The fox entered the Shard building through a central stairwell before climbing to the top Photo: HEATHCLIFF O'MALLEY/PA

Print this article | Share | Facebook | Twitter | Email | LinkedIn | +1 1

How about that?
News » UK News » Steven Swinford »

Elsewhere

Pictures of the day

UK's credit rating at risk after Osborne's debt failure

In How About That?

FREE MATTRESS
NO VISIBLE STAINS

By Steven Swinford
7:00AM GMT 25 Feb 2011

Staff discovered the intrepid visitor on the 72nd floor of the Shard building at London Bridge, 944ft above the ground.

The animal, nicknamed Romeo by staff, entered the building through a central stairwell before climbing to the top. It was living off scraps left by builders.

Pest controllers from Southwark Council eventually caught the fox after two weeks and took it to an animal sanctuary. It has since been released near London Bridge.

The fox was first spotted by a crane driver at the beginning of the month. Les Leonard, a pest controller, said: "At first I didn't believe it was up there, I thought it must be a hoax. I've got a fear of heights and getting the hoist lift from the 35th floor to the 72nd was terrifying.

"On the second day it ran straight past us then scrambled up a 10 foot ladder onto the rafters. It was surreal, we couldn't believe that a fox could go that high."

---

creare nell'area di Southwark un punto d'attrazione per il rilancio della città oltre il fiu-

Venite a meditare sul tetto di Londra

L'architetto Renzo Piano ci ha portato a vedere il suo nuovo grattacielo The Shard, che sarà pronto per le Olimpiadi. Accompagnandoci fino in cima, dove c'è una stanza molto particolare

di **Aldo Cazzullo** / Foto di **Steve Forrest**

La nuova opera

Tower Hill
Lower Thames St
Southwark St
London Bridge
Shard London Bridge
Borough
Southwark
Leathermarket St
Londra

...ma meta obbligata del nuovo turismo. Se il *Gherkin* è inaccessibile ai cittadini per ragioni di sicurezza, lo *Shard* dovrebbe al contrario funzionare da grande calamita, soprattutto ora che Londra si apre ad accogliere milioni di visitatori per le Olimpiadi.

Sfide Giovedì apre la torre di Renzo Piano: «Basta periferie tristi, le città devono includere. E alzarsi»

Una scheggia nel cuore di Londra

Il grattacielo «ecologicamente corretto» (solo 48 parcheggi)

dal nostro corrispondente
FABIO CAVALERA

LONDRA — Viva i grattacieli? O abbasso i grattacieli? Se lo chiediamo al principe Carlo, custode ultraortodosso dell'urbanistica inglese di stampo vittoriano, la risposta è scontata. Fosse per lui tutto ciò che va oltre il secondo piano sarebbe da cancellare. Picconi e ruspe.

Il giorno della regata storica sul Tamigi per il giubileo di sua maestà, passando davanti alla *Scheggia* sulla riva sud, il futuro re ha voltato la testa dall'altra parte, verso la City, forse dimenticando per un attimo che anche su quella sponda un siluro di vetro e acciaio a forma di *Cetriolo*, e tale è il suo simpatico soprannome, da un po' di anni si alza a ombreggiare la cattedrale di St. Paul. Per Carlo, ormai, risalire le acque limacciose del fiume deve essere un incubo visto come cambia il profilo della sua adorata città.

Invece, «Mummy» Elisabetta, che nonostante tutto è una signora al passo dei tempi, ha osservato a lungo, attratta e incantata, l'ultimo arrivato fra i palazzi che scalano il cielo londinese: la *Scheggia*, la *Shard* nel South Bank un tempo area di povertà, è il nuovo simbolo della capitale,

L'artista

◆ Nato a Pegli (Genova) nel 1937, Renzo Piano è stato il secondo architetto italiano (dopo Aldo Rossi) a vincere ...emio Pritzker ... Architetto ...tile hi-tech, ...reato al ...tecnico di ...ano nel 1964, ...no divenne ...noso nel 1971 ...ndo, con ...hard Rogers, ...truì il Centro ...mpidou ...arigi ... Nel 1988 ...omune di ...nova gli affida ...arico ...strutturare ...orto Antico, ...ista delle ...ebrazioni ...ombiane. Nel ...92, gli viene ...dato l'incarico ...costruire ...ea di ...sdamer Platz ...erlino dopo la ...nolizione del ...ro. Del 2002 ...Auditorium ...co della ...sica di Roma. ...la foto: Piano ... la maglietta ...e si legge «Trust me, I'm an architect»

di Renzo Piano, quando salivano in vetta anziché prendere i montacarichi se la sbrigavano a piedi «per tenersi in forma») e che è venuta su con tecnica «top-down» (i montatori salivano e parallelamente i minatori scendevano per le fondamenta) dopo la scoperta e la catalogazione per i musei dei resti di una villa romana del secondo secolo avanti Cristo che era persa lì sotto.

La *Scheggia* è una megacittà che vivrà 24 ore su 24 nei suoi 87 piani dei quali 72 destinati a uffici (fino al ventottesimo), a ristoranti (dal 31 al 33), ad alberghi (dal 34 al 52), ad abitazioni private (dal 53 al 65), a galleria, la Gallery View con balconata (dal 68 al 72) da dove o galleggerà al di sopra delle nuvole o si osserverà il panorama a 360 gradi in una profondità di sessanta miglia. E in cima, proprio in cima, la sorpresa: la «meditation room», una piccola stanza per riunioni riservate, a due passi dal paradiso o all'inferno.

Qui sopra e in alto lo «Shard» di Piano, nel South Bank di Londra

Allora architetto, evviva o abbasso i grattacieli? Renzo Piano ha con Londra un rapporto speciale: è da qui, tutto sommato, che ha mosso i primi passi con Richard Rogers, altra star della professione. E a lui nel 2000 l'allora sindaco Ken Livingstone, il laburista rosso, si rivolse spedendogli un emissario a Berlino dove stava lavorando alla ricostruzione post Muro e post guerra fredda. L'incontro in un ristorante vicino a Potsdamer Platz. L'idea è semplice: Londra non può espandersi oltre alla «green belt», la cintura verde è il limite naturale e di legge allo sviluppo urbanistico, dunque si tratta di inventare qualcosa di nuovo.

Spiega Renzo Piano che «il concetto di crescita cambia e, anziché costruire periferie tristi, pianeti suburbani che sono la negazione della vita sociale, le città si densificano intervenendo sui terreni compromessi delle ex ferrovie, delle ex caserme, delle ex fabbriche. L'etica del progetto *Shard* è proprio questa, Londra che non si allarga a macchia d'olio semmai che include e che si alza, nel massimo rispetto dell'ambiente e con forti risparmi energetici».

È una rivoluzione per la capitale inglese, gelosa del suo profilo lineare e basso. «I grattacieli godono di meritata pessima reputazione, sono a volte arroganti oggetti di potere e di speculazione. Occorre renderli fruibili da parte di tutti». Luoghi di lavoro e luoghi di divertimento che si muovono a ciclo continuo. La *Scheggia* prende forma in uno schizzo disegnato da Renzo Piano, buttato giù d'istinto. Il nome viene adottato nello studio, un «gergo familiare e informale dell'ufficio» di cui Londra si impossessa. La *Scheggia* di cristallo tradotta, diviene la *Shard*. Così piace. Così si eleva, dalla posa della prima pietra, al ritmo di due centimetri all'ora. E così è pronta.

«Una torre che non deve essere ostile e arrogante ma sottile», pianificò nel 2000 l'architetto. L'amministrazione londinese gli chiese di non progettare parcheggi (ve ne sono solamente 48) per disincentivare l'uso del mezzo privato e poi perché alla base della *Scheggia* c'è la London Bridge Station che ha un'utenza giornaliera di 300 mila persone, pendolari scaricati da due linee metropolitane, da sei linee ferroviarie, da 20 linee di bus. Una scelta di fondo: i quindicimila (tanti saranno) abitanti o clienti o lavoratori della *Scheggia* useranno i trasporti pubblici. Un grattacielo finanziato da un investitore privato ma «di valenza pubblica», come tiene a sottolineare Renzo Piano, per come è stato concepito, per l'appoggio dell'amministrazione, per la funzionalità che avrà, infine, per i criteri sofisticati di costruzione, «ecologicamente corretti».

La *Scheggia* assottigliandosi scherza col sole e coi riflessi.

La struttura

Sono 87 piani, 72 destinati a uffici. Ci sono alberghi, ristoranti e, in cima, una stanza per la meditazione

«Non è mai lo stesso edificio». Essendo in realtà composta da otto schegge che non s'incrociano e che ricevono i raggi in tempi e inclinazioni diversi, la torre non è illuminata sulle sue facce allo stesso modo. Si crea una magia visiva. «È lo specchio di questa Londra civile». Icona del secondo millennio (con firma italiana) che neppure la crisi finanziaria del 2008 ha fermato, segno che le idee marciano comunque quando sono forti. Anche l'*Empire State Building* di New York si alzò in tempi di crisi profonda. Ed è entrato nella storia del costume e della vita. Il principe Carlo un giorno si convincerà: non è narcisismo distruttivo, è elegante innovazione che non ferisce l'ambiente.

@fcavalera

© RIPRODUZIONE RISERVATA

Londres dispose de sa tour Eiffel

Signée Renzo Piano, elle dépasse son modèle parisien et devient la plus haute d'Europe

Architecture

Londres
Envoyé spécial

Du 6 au 10 juillet, la tour Shard, à Londres, la plus haute d'Europe, entrera progressivement en usage. Elle dépasse de quelques mètres la tour Eiffel qui, érigée en 1889 à l'occasion de l'Exposition universelle, était avant tout un symbole, censée être provisoire, mais qui avait trouvé son utilité, paysagère, gastronomique et radiophonique, grâce à une batterie d'antennes à son sommet.

La tour Shard joue sur un autre registre, même si sa construction coïncide aussi avec une grande cérémonie internationale, les JO de Londres 2012. Ses 306 mètres de hauteur offrent 40 000 m² de surface utile : bureaux, hôtel, plate-forme panoramique (accessible au public d'ici quelques semaines).

Non loin de la Tour de Londres, elle se trouve à cheval sur la gare de London Bridge, où convergent plusieurs lignes de train, de métro et de bus. Comme la Tate Modern, elle est venue s'installer dans un quartier naguère industriel ou déshérité. La tour Shard ne représente pas qu'elle-même. Toute la zone sud de la Tamise devrait bénéficier de son ombre.

Huit hautes écailles

Une ombre discrète : Renzo Piano a dessiné une tour dont l'épaisseur s'amenuise au fur et à mesure qu'elle s'élève. Le principe même de la tour Eiffel, qui, de ce fait, n'envahit pas l'espace aérien. Sa façade est composée de huit hautes écailles planes, blanches, nacrées, lumineuses, chacune prenant le relais au passage du soleil. Renzo Piano applique ici à la perfection ses meilleures recettes, la principale étant de se parer d'une élégance sobre sans être pauvre, ce qui est le moins que pouvaient souhaiter les quatre banques du Qatar qui ont financé la tour.

De son sommet, on découvre la complexité du paysage londonien, la frénésie architecturale de la City, ses parcs immenses, ses ports, son éclectisme à l'œuvre depuis la crise postmoderne des années 1980 et la montée au créneau du prince Charles, passionné de style corinthien. Les Jeux olympiques ajoutent à ces caractéristiques une dose de pragmatisme : peu d'architecture innovante, mais beaucoup de noms prestigieux. Le Centre aquatique, où se dérouleront les épreuves de natation, tire son épingle du jeu. C'est Zaha Hadid, architecte anglo-irakienne immensément célèbre, qui en a imaginé la forme : quelque chose comme un calamar géant, dont les volutes et la symétrie rappellent étrangement le vocabulaire de Santiago Calatrava, architecte de tours et de ponts très apprécié des maîtres d'ouvrage parce qu'il raconte des histoires simples.

La tour Shard, à Londres.
KEVIN COOMBS/REUTERS

Mais c'est dans Hyde Park que les étudiants en architecture viennent par centaines visiter ce qu'ils espèrent être le must de leur pèlerinage londonien : le pavillon provisoire (fermeture et destruction le 14 octobre) confié cette année aux architectes suisses Herzog et de Meuron (les auteurs du chef-d'œuvre de la Tate Modern). A leur nom est accolé celui d'Ai Weiwei, artiste et architecte chinois dissident, toujours assigné à résidence à Pékin. Comment ces trois architectes, qui ont construit le stade olympique de Pékin 2008, sont-ils parvenus à travailler ensemble sur ce minuscule bout de monument – un petit plan d'eau plus ou moins circulaire placé en lévitation au-dessus d'une sorte de cave archéologique imaginaire ?

Les étudiants se consoleront en visitant, au Victoria and Albert Museum, l'exposition consacrée à Heatherwick Studio, l'agence qui avait dessiné le spectaculaire pavillon anglais de l'Exposition universelle de Shanghaï. ■

Frédéric Edelman

Oggi è il 10 ottobre 2012: parliamo di London Bridge Tower, lo 'Shard'. Tutto è cominciato nel 2000 con una telefonata di Tony Fitzpatrick, un ingegnere strutturista di Arup oggi purtroppo scomparso. Ci avvisava che un importante imprenditore inglese, Irvine Sellar, voleva costruire un edificio a Londra, sopra la stazione di London Bridge.

Si tratta della più antica stazione della città, aperta nel 1836 a Southwark, subito a sud-est del London Bridge. Per me già l'idea di lavorare su un *brownfield*, ovvero una zona urbana dismessa e destinata alla riqualificazione, era interessante.

Si trattava di un tema molto sentito da Ken Livingstone, allora Sindaco di Londra, che aveva rilanciato il concetto di *green belt*: un invisibile confine verde intorno alla città che ne costituisce il limite di espansione. Così si impedisce che la città cresca in modo esplosivo e disomogeneo, erodendo le campagne circostanti e intaccando la zona verde. L'idea è invece che debba crescere per implosione, occupando le zone dismesse.

Oggi in Inghilterra è fortemente incoraggiato lo sfruttamento di terreni già edificati in precedenza, e poiché l'Inghilterra è stata la patria della rivoluzione industriale, è piena di *brownfields*. Tra queste zone ovviamente spiccano gli edifici industriali e ferroviari in disuso.

C'erano quindi i presupposti perché diventasse un lavoro interessante. Organizzammo un primo incontro a Berlino nel maggio del 2000, ricordo che eravamo in un ristorante di Marlene Dietrich Platz, nel centro di Potsdamer Platz.

Un luogo che per me ha un significato professionale particolare: il mio studio ha lavorato al progetto di riqualificazione urbana di quell'area per otto anni, dal 1992 al 2000.

Ho notato che talvolta i miei progetti si rincorrono l'un l'altro, è come se ci fosse una specie di staffetta in cui si passano il testimone. Queste fortunate coincidenze che collegano fra loro lavori anche diversissimi si sono verificate piuttosto spesso, forse è anche il semplice risultato di una lunga carriera.

In quella occasione incontrai per la prima volta Irvine Sellar. Un vero *self made man*: ha iniziato la sua carriera negli anni Sessanta vendendo abiti, fino a diventare uno dei grandi protagonisti della *Swinging London*. Ha ideato e costruito il riferimento per tutti i mercati alternativi del mondo: Carnaby Street che con i suoi negozi di musica indipendente, i Beatles e stilisti come Mary Quant ha cambiato il volto dell'Inghilterra. Scoprii che Irvine Sellar aveva affittato nel 1998 il terreno da Network Rail (la società privata derivata dalla British Rail) ed aveva già in mano un progetto di massima. Non era però del tutto soddisfatto, perché trovava che mancasse una visione precisa, che non rappresentasse un'idea forte. Per questo volle incontrarmi, ed iniziammo a discuterne insieme.

It's October 10th 2012: I'm talking about London Bridge Tower, often referred to as the *Shard*.

The project began in 2000 with a phone call from Tony Fitzpatrick, a structural engineer for Arup, who has since sadly passed away. He told us that a British entrepreneur, Irvine Sellar, wanted to construct a building in London above London Bridge railway station. The station, London's oldest, was inaugurated in 1836 in Southwark, just south-east of London Bridge. For me, the idea of working on a *brownfield* site, (an abandoned urban area destined for redevelopment), was an intriguing one. Ken Livingstone, at that time Mayor of London, had taken the issue to heart. In fact Livingstone had been working to give new impetus to the existing concept of the *green belt*: a green 'border' around London that constitutes its outer limit and on which building is strictly limited. It serves to prevent the city from growing explosively and unevenly, eroding the surrounding countryside. Instead the idea was that London should grow inwards, making use of the city's vacant sites. Today, construction in England is encouraged on land that has been previously developed, and since England was the birthplace of the Industrial Revolution, brownfield sites are not hard to come by. And naturally some of the most high profile of these areas include abandoned industrial and railway buildings.

The job was already starting to sound interesting!

Our initial meeting, in May 2000, was held at a restaurant in Berlin's Marlene Dietrich Platz, at the centre of Potsdamer Platz. It was a place that held particular meaning for me as a professional, as my office had been working on the area's urban redevelopment for eight years, from 1992 to 2000.

I've noticed that my projects sometimes seem to follow on from one another, as if they were in a kind of relay in which the baton is passed from one to the next. Fortuitous coincidences that sometimes link projects seem to happen to me quite often. Perhaps it's just the natural result of having a long career!

It was at that time that I first met Irvine Sellar. A true *self-made man*, he began his career in the 1960s selling clothes, and went on to become one of the great protagonists of *Swinging London*. He conceived of and built the reference point for all the world's alternative markets: Carnaby Street. With its independent music shops, the Beatles and designers like Mary Quant, it changed the face of England itself.

I found out that Irvine Sellar had leased the site at London Bridge in 1998 from Network Rail (the private company derived from British Rail), and already had a rough draft for a project in hand. He wasn't entirely satisfied however, because he felt that it lacked a clear vision and didn't convey a strong

L'idea alla base prese forma quasi subito, anche se non è vero che io quel giorno ho tracciato uno schizzo ed avevo già chiaro in mente come sarebbe stato il progetto.

Non vorrei alimentare una leggenda troppo semplicistica. È invece vero che iniziai a disegnare con il pennarello verde sul tavolo del ristorante, e ricordo anche che ad un certo punto il cameriere ci fece notare che la tovaglia era di lino.

In quel primo schizzo l'edificio non aveva la forma definitiva, ma alcuni elementi erano già chiari. Intanto che sarebbe stata una torre, il che era evidente da subito visto che l'area a disposizione a terra era limitata. E poi che doveva essere una piccola città verticale, con molte funzioni diverse e pochi posti auto. Quest'ultima era una delle felici imposizioni della municipalità di Londra: Ken Livingstone infatti ha introdotto la *congestion charge*, il pedaggio per entrare in città in auto che ha ridotto il traffico almeno del 30 per cento.

L'edificio si trova sopra la stazione di London Bridge, una delle più frequentate di Londra, che vede passare più di 50 milioni di passeggeri l'anno. È una stazione che ha la funzione di interscambio, un *transportation hub*: ci sono due metropolitane in profondità (Jubilee e Northern line), e poi quindici binari ferroviari e altrettante linee di autobus. È un sistema di trasporti straordinariamente sviluppato, che serve tra l'altro le contee sud orientali del paese.

Anche per questo è stato chiaro già dall'inizio che ci sarebbero stati pochissimi posti auto: alla fine sono diventati 48 per un edificio che ospiterà 8.000 persone.

Quel giorno a pranzo fu chiaro che le funzioni dovevano essere miste: innanzitutto c'era il trasporto pubblico già esistente, e le funzioni collegate ad esso, compresa quella commerciale.

Non sto parlando di uno shopping center, ma semplicemente delle piccole attività che si associano normalmente ad un grande snodo di trasporti. In effetti l'area interessata dall'operazione è stata alla fine molto più estesa: oltre allo Shard è stata coinvolta la stazione degli autobus di fronte a London Bridge ed una serie di interventi negli spazi pubblici intorno ad essa. Abbiamo anche ridisegnato la stazione di London Bridge: ora è più aperta e accessibile, un luogo che esprime meglio il rituale quotidiano dell'arrivare e del ripartire.

Alla fine del cantiere l'area prenderà il nome di London Bridge Quarter. Tutto questo prese subito forma in uno schizzo che non coincide con la forma finale, ma testimonia la chiarezza di intenti già dall'inizio. Pensavamo a un edificio con una base ampia che si assottiglia crescendo e finisce nel nulla. L'area a terra doveva essere pressoché interamente occupata dalla stazione, che aveva bisogno di molto spazio, e salendo la superficie diminuiva per ospitare gli uffici, i ristoranti, l'albergo e gli appartamenti. Quindi sostanzialmente la forma piramidale che si stringe salendo era già abbastanza chiara dall'inizio: la superficie a terra è di circa 4000 metri quadrati, la piattaforma panoramica quasi sulla cima è meno di 350.

Racconto questo per spiegare che il mito dell'intuizione tout court non esiste. È vero che il progetto prese forma rapidamente, ma non in una rivelazione improvvisa, piuttosto durante i primi mesi di lavoro, quando con una certa "spensieratezza" pensammo di fare un edificio con una forma così inclinata.

message. So he decided that he wanted to meet me, and we began to talk about the project. Although the basic idea began to take shape almost immediately, it's not true that I drew up a sketch that same day and had a clear idea of what the project would be like. I don't want to further compound that overly simplistic legend. It is however true that I began drawing on the restaurant's table with a green marker, and I remember that at one point the waiter pointed out that the tablecloth was made of linen. Although the building's final form was not entirely defined by that initial sketch, some of its core elements had already emerged. For example, given the limited amount of available space on the ground, we realised immediately that the building was to be a tower. It would be like a small vertical city, combining a mix of uses with limited car parking.

This latter characteristic was one of the constraints imposed upon the project by the city authorities: it was Ken Livingstone, in fact, who had introduced the *congestion charge*, the toll for entering the city by car, which went on to reduce traffic in central London by at least 30 per cent.

The building is situated above London Bridge Station, one of London's busiest railway stations with over 50 million passengers passing through each year. It's a station that serves as an interchange, or rather a *transportation hub*.

There are 2 underground lines (the Jubilee and Northern lines), 15 railway platforms, and 15 bus routes.

It's an extremely well-developed part of the overall transportation system, serving the south-east of England. That's another reason why it was evident from the beginning that there would be very few parking spaces. As it turned out, there would only be 48 spaces for a building that would be destined to host 8,000 people. That day at lunch, it became obvious that it would have to be a mixed-use building.

For a start there was the existing transportation hub, plus all the functions related to it, including commercial ones.

I'm not talking about a shopping centre, but simply the range of small businesses that are normally associated with a major railway station. In fact, the area that would be affected by our project was ultimately much more extensive: in addition to the Shard, the bus station in front of London Bridge station also became part of the development, including a series of interventions and public spaces surrounding it. We even reconfigured London Bridge station: it's now more open and accessible, and has become a place that better expresses the daily ritual of arriving and departing. The whole area is now known as the 'London Bridge Quarter'. All of this immediately took shape in a sketch that did not represent a definitive design, but that bore witness to the clarity of our intent from the outset. We envisioned a building with a broad base that would taper as it rose, until it disappeared. The street and concourse levels would be as small as possible to free up public space and space for the transport interchange.

The first office floors would then fill the site and as the building rose the surface area of each floor would decrease to house the restaurants, hotels and apartments. A pyramidal shape that narrows as it rises was therefore an evidence right away; the surface area at ground level is about 4000 square metres, while the viewing platform near the top is less than 350.

Quello che emerse durante le prime riflessioni, che erano di carattere decisamente più funzionale, era l'idea di una piccola città verticale con tante funzioni diverse. Una metafora felice, perché è bello immaginare uno spazio che vive 24 ore al giorno, esattamente come una porzione di città, un quartiere ben fatto, dove si mescolano residenze e lavoro, ed è sempre abitato.

E già quel giorno si iniziò a parlare di un luogo per la gente: d'altra parte eravamo in Marlene Dietrich Platz, che è una piccola piazza dove oggi le due Berlino, quella est e quella ovest, si sono ritrovate.

Si parlò dell'aspetto sociale e politico, del senso di appartenenza ad una *polis* come Londra, con la sua forte presenza storica di edifici, con la vicinanza al Tamigi.

E anche di poesia. In qualche modo ci dovevamo chiedere che senso avesse fare una torre così alta vicino al fiume, dove poco più di un secolo fa attraccavano ancora i velieri.

È stato un inizio piuttosto tormentato, come succede per quasi tutti i progetti, perché vi confluivano molti aspetti di tipo diverso. Anche quelli urbanistici, legati all'idea di una crescita più sostenibile, costruendo sul costruito e trasformando i luoghi secondo metamorfosi, attraverso una mutazione che ha reso le città europee luoghi così straordinari, come diagrammi visibili delle stratificazioni storiche che si sono succedute.

E non dimenticare l'aspetto scientifico: come progettare un edificio che consumi poco, e che provi la tesi che costruire alto ma concentrato in realtà è più sostenibile che costruire basso ma disperso? Perché fare edifici bassi sembrerebbe un gesto meno arrogante, più modesto e umile.

Peccato che sul piano dei consumi questo significhi l'opposto: intanto perché si occupa molto più territorio e la città che ne risulta è vastissima, con enormi distanze da coprire, servizi da spostare e periferie gigantesche.

Insomma, al di là dell'idea romantica di "villaggio" come luogo sostenibile, in realtà è vero il contrario: un edificio alto e compatto, che occupa poco terreno, e anzi lo restituisce alla città facendone delle piazze e degli spazi aperti e disponibili, se è concepito bene consuma meno energia ed è più sostenibile.

Questo finalmente sta diventando chiaro, tanto è vero che il mensile del Times ha aperto un dibattito sul tema, e persino una città come Los Angeles si sta muovendo sulla strada della concentrazione dei volumi e sul trasporto pubblico.

Quindi avevamo in mente anche la sfida di costruire una torre tecnicamente capace di provare questo assunto.

In genere nel progettare gli edifici alti si assume un atteggiamento "difensivo". Difensivo perché le torri devono letteralmente proteggersi, soprattutto dal caldo. Le radiazioni solari creano problemi di raffreddamento, persino in una città come Londra. Ma come si fa a proteggere un edificio evitando di ricorrere ai tradizionali vetri scuri, che producono facciate così ermetiche? È una delle ragioni per cui spesso i grattacieli appaiono così antipatici e aggressivi, perché sono oggetti estranei al contesto.

La nostra risposta è stata quella di lavorare su un sistema dinamico. Joost (Joost Moolhuijzen, partner RPBW capoprogetto dello Shard) ti racconterà come abbiamo fatto. Si tratta sostanzialmente di una facciata a "doppia pelle" con tende interne – collegate a sensori sensibili alla

The reason I'm telling you this is to explain that the design was not simply instinctive. It is true that the project took shape quickly, but not by means of a sudden revelation. Rather, it was during the first months of the work that we serendipitously conceived of a building that took this form. What came out of these early reflections, which were of a practical nature, was the concept of a small vertical city with a wide range of different functions. The vertical city was a good metaphor, because we liked the idea of a place that would be alive 24 hours a day, just like a part of the city: a well-built district that through a mix of residential and commercial spaces would be used around the clock. And that same day we also began talking about a meeting place for people, after all, we were in Marlene Dietrich Platz, a small square where east and west Berlin were reunited.

We talked about the social and political significance of belonging to a *polis* like London, with its abundance of historic buildings along the banks of the River Thames. And we even talked about poetry. We asked ourselves how it would be to site such a tall tower so close to the river, where less than a century ago sailboats had moored.

It was a rather complex beginning, as with many projects, because there were so many aspects to consider.

These included a sustainable model for urban growth and development; the successful reinvention and transformation of urban sites that has rendered so many European cities such extraordinary places, where the layers of their development are clearly visible, like diagrams of their history.

And let's not forget the technical aspect too. How does one design a building that consumes little energy and prove the theory that building a tall, concentrated structure is actually more sustainable than building low-rise? Because although it might seem less arrogant, more modest and humble to build low buildings, in terms of consumption the exact opposite would be true. Low buildings have much more surface area, and, if you keep on building like this, the resulting city would be vast with extensive outlying areas and suburbs, huge distances across which services and people need to be moved.

In short, the romantic idea of the 'village' as a sustainable place is not really true. A tall and compact building takes up little space on the ground, and even provides the surrounding city with additional space by creating squares and open spaces. Furthermore, if well designed, it will consume less energy and be more sustainable. This is finally becoming clear; in the press the Times newspaper has debated the issue, and even a city like Los Angeles is beginning to focus more on concentrated volumes and public transport. So we were also considering the challenge of building a tower that would be technically capable of proving this hypothesis.

In designing tall buildings, one typically assumes a *defensive* attitude. I say defensive because towers literally need to protect themselves, above all against heat. The heat from solar radiation (sunshine) can surprisingly even be an issue in London. But how can a building be protected without resorting to the use of traditional tinted windows, which result in opaque façades? This is one of the reasons that skyscrapers can appear aggressive and unappealing, because they don't communicate

luce – che scendono sulle facciate esposte direttamente alle radiazioni. Con questo sistema la torre si sarebbe trasformata continuamente. Bisognava realizzarlo tecnicamente, provandolo e testandolo, ma al di là della riuscita dal punto di vista termico, abbiamo capito che funziona molto bene anche dal punto di vista della presenza dell'edificio, che diventa metamorfico, cambia continuamente, è in movimento. Una torre che gioca con la luce.

Accanto a questo aspetto di carattere più scientifico ce n'era uno formale: ricordiamoci che parliamo di un edificio da costruire non lontano dalla Tower of London e dalla cattedrale di St. Paul, che si trova sull'altra riva del Tamigi. D'altronde il quartiere di Southwark è il cuore della città antica, Londra è nata lì, e il London Bridge è stato il primo ponte della città, l'unico sul Tamigi a valle di Kingston fino al 1700. Durante gli scavi ci sono stati due ritrovamenti archeologici: il primo nel 2011, una villa romana del II sec. A.C., e il secondo pochi giorni fa, sul cantiere della London Bridge House, un edificio per uffici progettato da noi che sta nascendo di fronte allo Shard.

Deve essere un destino perché anche a Roma, durante gli scavi dell'Auditorium Parco della Musica inaugurato proprio dieci anni fa, trovammo resti archeologici. Ma a Roma è quasi inevitabile, mentre a Londra per me è stata una sorpresa. La villa romana è stata attentamente rilevata da esperti del Museum of London, ed ovviamente i reperti sono stati recuperati. Quindi insieme agli aspetti politici, urbanistici, scientifici e tecnologici c'erano anche aspetti storici che confluivano ad alimentare il processo progettuale.

Come succede sempre, in ogni progetto. Ma qui forse in maniera più complessa, perché le scommesse erano importanti: fare una torre che consumasse poca energia, e dimostrare che una città può crescere e intensificarsi senza alimentare nuove periferie. E considera che all'inizio l'edificio doveva essere più alto: 400 metri. Poi lo abbassammo perché la rotta di atterraggio degli aerei impediva un'altezza simile. Ma anche scendendo a 306 metri avremmo comunque costruito la torre più alta di Londra, e senz'altro la più visibile. Nella zona dello Shard oltretutto c'è un solo edificio di circa 120 metri: è la sede del Guy's Hospital. Era evidente quindi che c'era una questione aperta: comunque la si voglia intendere si trattava infatti di costruire una torre che sarebbe potuta apparire un'arrogante sfida alla città, una prepotenza. E allora capimmo che la necessità funzionale di diventare sempre più sottile in alto si sposava a quella di alleggerire l'edificio, renderlo una presenza tesa, sottile e tagliente. L'aspetto "morfologico" della torre è derivato in uguale misura da scelte di tipo funzionale e di tipo tecnico-scientifico. Quest'idea di salire in maniera sottile e lentamente sparire nel cielo evocava un'immagine familiare della città. Ci sono celebri paesaggi del Canaletto, che visse a lungo a Londra, che rappresentano il Tamigi da cui si sollevano spire di fumo e emergono le guglie degli edifici. E a me in qualche modo venivano in mente anche gli alberi delle navi che secoli fa attraccavano lì davanti, pensa ai *clipper* che arrivavano dall'Australia nel Settecento e Ottocento. Ne parlo con molta cautela perché sarebbe banale dire che la forma definitiva

with their surrounding context. Our answer was to make use of a dynamic facade system. Joost (Joost Moolhuijzen, RPBW partner for the Shard) explains in more detail how we did it. It's basically a *double-skin façade* with internal blinds. Light sensors lower the blinds when the sun shines on that particular façade of the building. This system would mean that visually, the tower would be continuously transforming. The facade had to be developed technically and then tried and tested. Beyond ensuring success in terms of heat economy, we also thought that this system would work well on an aesthetic level, allowing the building to metamorphose, the appearance of its facades changing and in motion: a tower that plays with the effects of the light. And in addition to these technical aspects, there were formal considerations to be made too. We had to remember that we were talking about a building to be constructed not far from the Tower of London and St. Paul's Cathedral, which is situated just across the Thames. The historic district of Southwark represents the heart of the ancient city. London Bridge was the city's first bridge over the river Thames and central London's only bridge until the 18th century. We unearthed two significant archaeological finds during the site preparations: the first, in 2011, was a Roman villa from the second century B.C. The second was discovered more recently on the site of London Bridge House, where an office building, also part of the scheme, is being erected opposite the Shard. It must be fate, because we also uncovered archaeological remains in Rome during the excavations for the Auditorium Music Park, inaugurated ten years ago. That seems almost inevitable in Rome, but in London it was quite a surprise for me. The Roman villa was carefully surveyed and excavated by specialists from the Museum of London and many artefacts were recovered.

So there were historical details to consider in addition to the political, technical and planning issues, when thinking about our design. While these are almost always factors in the design of a building here they were made more complex because of the significant challenge of building a low energy tower and having to prove the theory that a city can grow successfully by building upon previously developed land. Originally the building was supposed to be taller: 400 m high! We lowered it because a building that tall posed issues for flight paths into London's airports. But even at 306 m, the building remains the tallest tower in London, and by far the most prominent. In the vicinity of the Shard there is just one other tall building: Guy's Hospital Tower, which is approximately 120 m tall. So there was another matter to be resolved; no matter how we looked at it, we were building a tower that could appear arrogant, a challenge to the city itself. And then we realised that organising the diverse functions inside the building so that it necessarily tapered towards the top would also help to make the building lighter, giving it an extended, narrow presence. The tower's morphology therefore is equally derived from the functional and technical choices that were made. This idea of the tower rising subtly and slowly disappearing into the sky evoked a familiar image of the city for me. There are famous landscape paintings by Canaletto, who lived in London for many years, showing the river Thames

è derivata da queste riflessioni, infatti stiamo parlando di dimensioni e di scale completamente diverse; ma indubbiamente l'idea di far diventare l'edificio sempre più sottile fino a rompersi nel cielo richiama questi paesaggi. Per questo in ufficio iniziammo a chiamarlo "the Shard": qualcuno usò il termine per definire le "scaglie" che componevano le facciate. È stata una sineddoche: una parte ha finito per definire il tutto. L'idea, che esisteva già prima che le trovassimo il nome di "Shard", cominciò a rivelarsi il modo giusto di interpretare questo desiderio formale: perché le scaglie quando arrivano in cima non si chiudono, restano aperte, come se respirassero. In qualche maniera aspirano a un punto che però non raggiungono. C'è un punto teorico, a circa 360 metri di altezza, in cui le facciate si sarebbero riunite se lo Shard avesse continuato a crescere.

Questa voglia di salire ancora fa parte del desiderio di trovare una forma che non fosse troppo certa, ma in qualche maniera "titubante". È il problema delle torri: spesso sono simboli di potere e di superbia, questa doveva essere invece qualcos'altro, una guglia che si frantuma in cielo, con le scaglie che hanno angoli diversi e che continuano a cambiare con i cambiamenti della luce. Un dettaglio che ha avuto una grande importanza è stata l'inclinazione delle facciate, perché se i vetri sono verticali riflettono ciò che hanno di fronte, ma se sono inclinati leggermente verso l'alto riflettono il cielo. Questa piccola constatazione significava una cosa: che l'edificio sarebbe stato meteorologico e fotosensibile, come un sensore del cielo. E il cielo di Londra è uno dei più mobili del mondo: le nuvole passano veloci, c'è la pioggia e poi il tempo cambia e torna il sole. È un cielo nordico, fluviale, e la torre in qualche maniera gli ruba quest'anima, essendone lo specchio. Certo, non uno specchio in senso letterale, perché non è in vetro riflettente, ma anche il vetro extra-white prende il colore del cielo e delle nuvole, e la sera al tramonto prende un tono più caldo. Questa considerazione venne immediatamente ad alimentarne un'altra di tipo formale: non solo l'edificio ha una forma "incerta" che sparisce nel cielo, ma anche il materiale è sensibile, e dato che la sfaccettatura è multipla, quando il sole gira una faccia diventa riflettente e l'altra no. Inoltre, visto che sulla facciata illuminata scendono le tende, a questo punto l'effetto cambia ancora. Se la giornata è grigia è tutto più pacato, se invece è soleggiata vedi solo una delle facciate e le altre spariscono, e la torre sembra un fantasma, non si capisce come faccia a stare in piedi. Quindi, a partire da quel pranzo a Berlino con Irvine Sellar, cominciò un processo che durò qualche mese, in cui tutti questi elementi vennero considerati insieme. Ed erano davvero tante cose, non semplicemente il risultato di uno schizzo tracciato sulla tovaglia.

Il problema era spiegarlo; perché finché ne parli a Ken Livingstone è una cosa, ma cambia se hai di fronte l'English Heritage o l'Historic Royal Palaces. E allora si aprì un capitolo piuttosto complesso, perché ci fu chi disse che lo Shard avrebbe messo in ombra St. Paul.

St. Paul è una straordinaria cattedrale, dalle proporzioni perfette, con la cupola di Christopher Wren così fragile e sottile. L'idea che un edificio a un chilometro e mezzo di distanza, dall'altra parte del Tamigi, potesse mettere in ombra

with coils of smoke and building spires rising above it. And for me the masts of the ships that docked there centuries before somehow came to mind, like the *Clippers* that arrived from Australia during the eighteenth and nineteenth centuries. I talk about this rather cautiously, as it would be trivial to say that the final form was derived from these considerations. In fact, we're talking about completely different sizes and scales. But the idea of rendering the building increasingly thin until it disintegrates into glass slivers in the sky is certainly reminiscent of these landscapes. That's why we began to refer to it as *the Shard* in the office; someone had used this term to describe the *slivers* that made up the building's facets. It was a synecdoche: a part that came to define the whole. The idea of the building disappearing into sky, which was already there before we came up with the name of the Shard, helped us to interpret this formal desire, because when the slivers arrive at the top, they aren't closed off, but remain open as if they were breathing, almost as if they are reaching for a point that they are unable to achieve. (There is a theoretical point, about 360 m up, where the facades would meet if the *Shard* were to continue to grow).

This aspiration to continue rising can be seen as part of our desire to come up with a form that was not too certain. We were looking for a form that would somehow appear hesitant. Because the problem with towers is that they're often symbols of power and pride. This one however was meant to be something else, a spire that would shatter into the sky with slivers of various angles, constantly changing with the variations of the light.

One significant detail was the tilt of the building's facades, because if the windows were to be positioned vertically they would reflect whatever was opposite them. If they were tilted slightly upwards on the other hand, they would reflect the sky. This small consideration meant one thing: that the building would be sensitive to changes in weather and light, like a sensor for the sky. And the London sky is one of the world's most interesting, the clouds pass by quickly, it rains and then the weather changes and the sun peeks through the clouds again. It's a fluid northern sky, and the tower somehow manages to harness its soul and reflect it. Not like a mirror, because it's not made of reflective glass, but even *extra-white* glass takes on the colour of the sky and the clouds, and assumes a warmer tone in the evening at sunset. As a result not only has the building taken on an "uncertain" form that disappears into the sky, but the material is sensitive as well, and given the multitude of surfaces of which it is comprised, one face becomes reflective as the sun turns, while the others do not. The blinds will create further effects. On a grey day, everything is calm. If it's sunny you only see one of the facades of the building while the others seem to disappear and it's hard to understand how it can remain standing. Beginning with that lunch in Berlin with Irvine Sellar, I embarked upon a process that would last several months, during which all of these elements were taken into consideration. And there were so many things involved, not just the sketch on a tablecloth. One problem was explaining the project, because it's one thing to talk to Ken Livingstone, but it's quite another to make a presentation to

St. Paul mi sembrava assurda, eppure ci fu chi la sostenne, e rapidamente le cose si complicarono.
Tra l'altro dimenticavano che quando la cattedrale fu costruita venne osteggiata ferocemente: pensa che il progetto di Wren fu rifiutato quattro volte. Quando fu costruita St. Paul era molto moderna, non era affatto un "classico", lo diventò solo molto tempo dopo. Fu deciso quindi da John Prescott, Vice-Primo Ministro, di fare una *Public Inquiry*, come avviene quando si deve decidere sulla realizzazione di grandi edifici, aeroporti e infrastrutture. Si tratta di un vero e proprio processo al progetto. Fu nominato un Ispettore, John Gray, con il quale ci confrontammo: discutendo, provando e riprovando, mettendo a punto. Capimmo rapidamente che, avendo interlocutori intelligenti (e come tali, talvolta, irritanti) la cosa non poteva che essere utile al progetto. Fu una procedura lunga e abbastanza provante, ma anche formativa, con una discussione accesa fra favorevoli e contrari. Va considerato che la legge inglese non applica i codici ma *common law*, in base alla quale l'insieme dei precedenti diventa legge, ed i casi simili sono valutati in maniera simile. E questo vale anche per l'urbanistica.
C'erano una commissione urbanistica speciale per i progetti più importanti nella città, la CABE, il GLA (Greater London Authority), e i servizi urbanistici di Southwark, il *Borough* di Londra diretto da Fred Manson, un uomo molto preparato. Ci fu un dibattito in rapporto con una visione della città. Non solo sul piano storico, per capire se l'edificio avrebbe disturbato o no il quadro complessivo, ma anche su quello urbanistico: ci si chiedeva cosa avrebbe dato alla città, cosa avrebbe cambiato.
Fu un'esperienza abbastanza interessante, ed anche doverosa per noi architetti che dovremmo essere consapevoli delle nostre responsabilità: facciamo un mestiere pericoloso per la comunità, e se ci sbagliamo il nostro errore rimane a lungo. Dovrebbe essere obbligatorio, purché naturalmente non si tratti di un procedimento troppo lungo e inconcludente. In questo caso durò sette mesi: dall'aprile a novembre 2003, e alla fine l'Ispettore dichiarò che si trattava di un progetto interessante e valeva la pena svilupparlo. E allo stesso tempo raccolse in un decalogo tutti gli elementi irrinunciabili per la corretta esecuzione. Con grande soddisfazione devo dire che quella lista coincideva con i presupposti che avevamo sviluppato: l'Ispettore aveva estratto le dieci cose che gli sembravano più interessanti e le aveva trasferite in un documento, in modo da difenderle da eventuali modifiche. Fra queste c'era ad esempio la caratteristica del vetro, che doveva essere a basso tenore di metallo, garantendo così che non potesse essere cambiato durante la realizzazione dell'edificio.
Il progetto nacque, come succede sempre, dal continuo alternarsi di tanti approci diversi: scientifico, storico, formale, artistico e espressivo, concentrandoci sulla visione della città e del futuro. Tutto questo processo durò almeno tre anni, poi ci fu un momento critico: i soci di Sellar abbandonarono il progetto, e lui dovette cercare nuovi finanziamenti.
Nel 2008 l'Emiro del Qatar ebbe un ruolo importante: fu lui ad intuire che lo Shard non era solo un'avventura commerciale o un simbolo, ma che rappresentava anche una visione del

English Heritage or Historic Royal Palaces. And then a rather difficult chapter began, because some people believed that the Shard would dominate St. Paul's Cathedral.
St. Paul's is an extraordinary cathedral with perfect proportions, boasting an incredibly thin and fragile dome designed by Sir Christopher Wren. The idea that a building 1.5 km away on the other side of the river Thames could dominate St. Paul's Cathedral seemed totally absurd, and yet there were those who supported it, and the situation soon became delicate. Many people had of course forgotten that the cathedral itself was fiercely opposed at the time of its construction.
It was considered to be out of scale, as well as an eyesore. Wren's draft designs were rejected four times. When St. Paul's was built, the design was very modern. It was not at all *classic*, and only became recognized as such much later.
Deputy Prime Minister, John Prescott, decided to hold a Public Inquiry, a process which often becomes necessary to make decisions about significant construction projects, such as major buildings, airports or other infrastructure projects. Our project was effectively put on trial. An Inspector, John Gray, was appointed, and we started a year and a half of legal proceedings aimed at discussing, proposing, re-proposing and adapting various aspects of the project. We quickly realized that since we were dealing with intelligent individuals - despite which, it was a long and often trying experience - the process would ultimately be beneficial to the project itself. It was also educational with a number of interesting debates between those who were in favour of the project and those who were against it. It should be noted that English law does not apply strict codes, but rather *common law*, under which all of the precedents are recognized as law, and similar cases are evaluated in a similar manner. There was a special urban planning commission, CABE, who looked at the city's most important projects; the GLA (Greater London Authority); and the planning team from the local London Borough of Southwark, headed by Fred Manson, an extremely capable man. Discussion ensued about a future vision for the city. What would the building add and what would it change? How would that impact on the historic fabric of London and what would it bring for the future?
It was an interesting experience, as well as one that we architects must recognize as our duty, as we must always be aware of our responsibilities. We perform a potentially dangerous task for the community, and if we get it wrong our error is around for a long time. Maybe it should be mandatory, as this would prevent many mistakes, provided of course that the process is not excessively long or inconclusive.
In our case, it lasted seven months: from April to November of 2003, and in the end the Inspector decided the project was interesting and saw its development as worthwhile. And at the same time he established a set of guidelines including all the essential elements for the project's proper execution.
I must say that I was quite pleased to see that the list coincided with the conditions that we ourselves had proposed.
The Inspector had taken the ten things that seemed most interesting and had transcribed them into a document, the *Decalogue*, in order to protect them against any future modifications.

futuro. La vicenda andò avanti abbastanza avventurosamente, finché riuscimmo ad aprire il cantiere nel 2009. Abbiamo avuto un ottimo team. Un gruppo numeroso: quasi 200 persone tra i nostri architetti RPBW, lo studio del local architect Adamson Associates, una buona impresa di costruttori (il gruppo Mace) e poi gli ingegneri di WSP e Arup, e i project managers del cliente. Il cantiere è stato grande, al momento culminante ci hanno lavorato 1.500 persone, di 60 nazionalità diverse. Ed è stato complesso, anche se lo abbiamo semplificato utilizzando per la prima volta per il nucleo di un edificio così alto la tecnica del *top down*. Funziona così: si realizza una piastra di cemento armato a piano terra, sorretta da pilastri piantati profondamente nel terreno. Quindi si scavano i piani interrati e contemporaneamente si costruisce in altezza. L'edificio cresce come un albero: mentre le radici attecchiscono il tronco cresce. E questo ci ha consentito di risparmiare molto tempo. In una torre alta 300 metri i piani interrati scendono di 20 e le fondazioni sono profonde 53: con questo sistema mentre la squadra dei minatori scendeva quella dei costruttori saliva. È un dato importante dal punto di vista scientifico, perché questo edificio ha spinto più avanti il processo costruttivo. Ad esempio il *core* è stato costruito con un sistema di casseformi che saliva progressivamente. Il nucleo è in cemento: il getto continuava sempre allo stesso ritmo, spostandosi di 4 millimetri al minuto, e la lentezza di salita consentiva che il cemento facesse presa via via. Questa operazione è andata avanti ininterrottamente per mesi, 24 ore al giorno per sei giorni alla settimana, con due team di operai che si davano il turno ogni 12 ore sulla piattaforma. Sulla carta sembra semplice, ma ti assicuro che non lo è: fatti raccontare da William com'è stato il cantiere (William Matthews, architetto associato RPBW).
Per capirne la straordinarietà basta guardare le foto: i pezzi che vengono montati a trecento metri di altezza, con raffiche di vento che possono arrivare a 70/80 chilometri all'ora.
La squadra che ha lavorato in alto era formata da alpinisti: li vedevo girare perfettamente equipaggiati con l'attrezzatura da scalata. Salivano 70 piani a piedi per allenarsi: erano gli unici a non usare gli ascensori di cantiere.
È successo di tutto: persino la cattura di una volpe urbana che era salita al settantaduesimo piano e ha vissuto lì per settimane, a più di 280 metri, mangiando i resti dei pranzi degli operai.
È stata un'esperienza straordinaria, ricca di momenti felici. L'attesa nelle fasi costruttive dello Shard è stata davvero forte. C'è sempre un'aspettativa, in ogni progetto. E qui era molto sentita, perché bisognava vedere quale sarebbe stata la presenza vera dell'edificio nella città, una volta raggiunta la sommità. E adesso che la sommità è stata raggiunta e la torre ha smesso di crescere è il momento di trarre qualche conclusione.
Le schegge di vetro arrivate in cima si fermano, e restano lì come sospese, ed era proprio l'effetto che speravo. E un'altra cosa che ho notato è che la torre è davvero molto meteorologica, durante il cantiere ho tenuto le dita incrociate, perché non sapevo esattamente come sarebbe finita. Per "finita" intendo proprio la fine, la sua sommità: che è la cosa più bella, fotosensibile come il resto. A seconda della distanza la torre cambia completamente. Da vicino sparisce, la prospettiva è accelerata, si vede solo un cristallo; da lontano è quasi sempre

These included, for example, the characteristics of the glass, which had to have a low iron content. The decalogue ensured that these key elements could not be changed during the building's construction. As you can see, the project came about from the continuous alternation of various different approaches: technical, historical, formal, artistic and expressive, focusing on a vision of the city. The entire process lasted three years, and was followed by a critical period, when Sellar's partners left the project and he sought new financing. In 2008 the Emir of Qatar took on an important role backing the project. He realized that the Shard would not be merely a commercial venture or a symbol, but also represented a vision of the future. The process then moved ahead again quickly, until we were finally able to begin construction in 2009.
We had a magnificent team on site. We were a large group of nearly 200 people: our own architects; the local architectural firm Adamson Associates; an excellent contractor, Mace Group; the engineers at WSP and Arup; and the client's project team. The site was extremely busy; at its peak there were up to 1500 workers of 60 different nationalities. The construction process itself was also complex, despite the fact that we simplified it by using a *top down* building technique for the first time for the core of a tall building. Top down construction works by pouring a slab of reinforced concrete on the ground floor. This is supported on plunge columns driven into the ground as foundations. You then dig out the first, second and third basement levels whilst simultaneously the core of the building is constructed above. In this manner, the building grows like a tree: the roots take hold as the trunk grows.
And this allowed us to save a lot of time. In our 300 m high tower, the basement is 20 m deep and the foundations are 53 m deep. As the team of excavators dug deeper, the team of builders continued to climb higher. From a technical standpoint, this building progressed construction techniques. Another example of this was the *slip formed* core that rose slowly but continuously, gaining 4 mm every minute. Made of concrete, it was poured at a constant speed, with the slow rate of ascent allowing the concrete to progressively set.
This operation continued for months, 24 hours a day, 6 days a week, with 2 teams of workers doing 12 hour shifts in the slip form rig. It might sound easy, but I can assure you that it is not: William (William Matthews, associate architect RPBW) will tell you more about how work progressed at the site.
You only have to look at the photographs to appreciate how impressive it was; elements of the building were assembled 300m above the ground, with gusts of wind reaching 70/80 km/h. The team that worked up at those heights was made up of professional climbers. I used to see them walking about fully equipped with their climbing gear. They climbed 70 floors on foot in order to train; they were the only ones who didn't use the site's elevators. For them, it was like climbing a 300 m rock face. They even captured an urban fox that had climbed up to the 72nd floor and had been living there for weeks, more than 280 m above the ground, eating the leftovers of the workers' meals. It was an extraordinary experience that left everyone with many great memories. However, the sense of expectation during the construction phase of the Shard was

molto bella, anche quando è grigia, dalla media distanza è interessante quando il sole batte su una delle facce e le altre spariscono. Ma lo Shard potrebbe ancora riservare qualche sorpresa, perché non è ancora completo.

Quando lo sarà funzioneranno i sistemi computerizzati che governano il movimento delle tende, e l'impressione cambierà ancora. Si tratta proprio di un movimento, perché le tende seguono la rotazione del sole che si sposta nell'arco della giornata. Aspetto quel momento per capire esattamente quale sarà l'effetto finale. Per ora posso dire che, fortunatamente, l'interno è luminosissimo, e questa luminosità è dovuta al fatto che il vetro non è né riflettente né oscurato, e la luce che entra è governata da un sistema attivo.

Certo, non è un progetto che lascia indifferenti, basta pensare alle reazioni della stampa. Sul Guardian negli ultimi mesi ci sono stati due articoli importanti. Il primo dice che distrugge Londra, paragonandoci ai talebani che a Timbuctù hanno distrutto le moschee e in Afghanistan i Buddha di Bamiyan. Gesto giustamente condannato come "tragedia per l'umanità" dall'Unesco.

Il secondo articolo, a distanza di un mese, dice che è l'edificio più bello di Londra dai tempi di St. Paul. Questa polarizzazione di opinioni è la tipica reazione ai progetti che rappresentano un cambiamento. Quando realizzi questo tipo di edifici, pensa anche al Centre Pompidou a Parigi, crei qualcosa di inatteso, e le cose inattese dividono l'opinione pubblica. L'idea stessa di trasformazione rende ansiosi. Il Pompidou agli inizi degli anni '70 rappresentò un momento di mutamento nella percezione degli edifici culturali: da luoghi chiusi e sacrali a luoghi aperti e accessibili. Oggi, allo stesso modo, lo Shard testimonia l'idea che si può intensificare la vita di una città anche costruendo in altezza. Rappresenta quindi un'idea urbana, e rende più riconoscibile una zona un po' dimenticata, seppure frequentatissima, di Londra.

Non so ancora come l'edificio sarà vissuto nel futuro, però vedo già come è percepito adesso. Circolano da tempo, su internet, siti web e *blog* che hanno testimoniato fotograficamente il cantiere, io li chiamo i "tower watchers". Ho l'impressione che la costruzione della torre sia stata vista con benevolenza, con curiosità, anche con un certo orgoglio. E il legame con la città sarà ancora più forte non appena ci si potrà salire e vedere da lassù lo spettacolo di Londra, l'edificio sarà amato anche perché sarà accessibile, non estraneo.

Una cosa che mi sembra importante è che lo Shard stia diventando un riferimento visivo importante nel quotidiano della città. London Bridge Station è il punto in cui il rituale di incontro tra la periferia e la città è più visibile: è un luogo di scambio naturale tra chi arriva a Londra dalla periferia, chi è di passaggio e chi invece in città vive e lavora. E questa torre sale in quel punto come un segnale. Quando a settembre tutto l'ufficio è stato a Londra per visitare l'edificio, molti hanno notato che in quella zona di Londra è diventato difficile perdersi, per ritrovare la strada è sufficiente guardare in alto. E guarda caso questo riferimento, come una specie di meda di orientamento che galleggia sulla città di Londra, non è nel cuore ricco di Londra, ma nella zona più popolare, a sud del Tamigi. In qualche modo lo Shard ha messo sulla mappa di

almost unbearable. With every project there is always a degree of nervous anticipation. And in this case it was utterly genuine because we were waiting to see what the building's actual presence in the city would be like once we reached the summit. And now that the summit has been reached and the tower has ceased to grow, we can finally draw some conclusions.

The uppermost shards of glass appear to stop, remaining there as if suspended, and this is precisely the effect that I was hoping to achieve. Another thing that I noticed is that the tower really is weather responsive. I kept my fingers crossed during construction because it was impossible to know exactly how it would end up. And by 'end' I am specifically referring to the top of the tower itself. It's the most beautiful thing, responding to changes in light just like the rest of the building.

Depending on your distance from the building the effects of light on the facades completely change the way the building looks. From close up it looks like a crystal, from far away the surfaces are always exceptionally beautiful, even when the weather is grey. And from midway between the two it's amazing to watch when the sun catches one of the faces of the building, making the other sides seem to disappear. And the Shard may hold further surprises. Once the computerized systems that handle the movements of the blinds are functioning the look of the building will change yet again because the blinds will follow the rotation of the sun as it moves across the sky throughout the day. I'm looking forward to that moment in order to get an idea of exactly what the final effect will be. For now, fortunately, I can say that the interior is very light because the glass is very transparent, and the light that enters the building will be managed by the dynamic facade system. It certainly wasn't a project that could have gone unnoticed. Just look at the reactions in the press. In the Guardian newspaper there have been two important articles in recent months. The first one says that the Shard destroys London, comparing us to the Taliban who destroyed the mosques in Timbuktu and the Bamiyan Buddhas in Afghanistan, (acts which were rightly condemned as 'tragedies for humanity' by UNESCO). The second article, published one month later, described it as the most beautiful building to be constructed in London since St. Paul's. This polarization of opinions is a typical reaction to projects that represent change. When you construct a building of this type, I am remembering the Centre Pompidou in Paris, you're creating something unexpected, and unexpected things tend to divide public opinion. The very idea of transformation makes people anxious. In the early 1970s the Pompidou represented a time in which the perception of cultural buildings was changing, from enclosed and sacred places, to open and accessible places. Today, in a similar manner, the Shard bears witness to the idea that building vertically can intensify the life of a city. It thus represents an urban concept, rendering a somewhat forgotten yet highly frequented part of London all the more recognizable. I still don't know how the building will be perceived in the future, but I can see what people think of it now. There have been websites and blogs on the Internet for some time which have provided a photographic account of the building's construction. I like to refer to these as 'tower watchers'. I get the impression that the tower's construction has

Londra questa parte della città, come era già nelle intenzioni dell'allora sindaco di Londra Ken Livingstone.

I suoi obiettivi più importanti erano due: il recupero dei *brownfields*, e l'equilibrio urbanistico tra la zona nord e quella sud di Londra. Mi disse che, volendo costruire un edificio "importante", che avrebbe potuto diventare emblematico, non lo avrebbe costruito nella *City*, ma al di là del fiume.

L'ultima volta che sono stato a Londra, adesso che il cantiere è finito, ho fatto quello che faccio sempre, tanto che ormai è diventata una mia consuetudine: ho spiato. Mi sono messo a camminare controcorrente su St. Thomas Street, in direzione opposta, guardando il viso della gente che mi veniva incontro scoprendo lo Shard.

Nella mia carriera ormai lunga sono arrivato persino a nascondermi dietro ai pilastri per vedere le reazioni delle persone agli edifici; stavolta invece la tecnica è stata di passeggiare facendo finta di telefonare, perché mi vergognavo a fissarle. E le ho viste avvicinarsi distratte, chiacchierando tra loro o semplicemente guardando altrove, e poi fermarsi un attimo e guardare in su. E le espressioni non erano mai di rifiuto, casomai di sorpresa e di gioia.

Renzo Piano, 2012

been viewed with kindness and curiosity, even a certain degree of pride. And this bond with the city will grow even stronger as soon as visitors have the chance to get up there and enjoy the spectacular view of London. At that point, the building will be much more highly appreciated, because it will have become accessible and will no longer be seen as just an object on the horizon. One thing that I consider important is the way that the Shard is gradually becoming a visual landmark for everyday life in the city. London Bridge Station is a place where the meeting point between the suburbs and the city is very visible; it's a place of natural exchange between those who are arriving in London from the suburbs, those who are passing through, and those who live and work in the city itself. And this tower stands precisely at that point like a signal. When our whole office went to London to see the building in September, many noticed that it was difficult to get lost in that area of London. To find your way, you just have to look for the Shard. And it just so happens that this visual reference point is not situated in the heart of the City of London but in a more mixed area, south of the river Thames. The Shard has put this part of the city on the map, just as Ken Livingstone had intended. Livingstone, in fact, had two major goals: first the reuse of brownfield sites and the densification of the city; second a new balance in urban planning between the northern and southern zones of London. He told me that he wanted to see an important building constructed that could potentially become emblematic, not in the City itself, but south of the river.

The last time I went to London, after the construction had been completed, I did what I always do, to the point that it has now become a habit: I spied. I walked against the crowd on St. Thomas Street, watching the faces of the people coming towards me looking up at the Shard. In my long career, I have even been known to hide behind pillars in order to watch people's reactions to our buildings. This time I adopted the technique of pretending to make a phone call, because I was embarrassed to stare at them. And I saw them approaching me distracted, chatting amongst themselves or simply looking away, and then stopping for a moment and looking upwards. And the expressions that I observed were not negative, but rather full of surprise and delight.

THE VIGWING GALLERY.

2000–2012
The London Bridge Tower
London, UK

Client: Sellar Property Group

Renzo Piano Building Workshop, architects
in collaboration with Adamson Associates
(Toronto, London)

Phase One (Planning Application), 2000-2003
Design team
J. Moolhuijzen (partner in charge),
N. Mecattaf, W. Matthews with D. Drouin,
A. Eris, S. Fowler, H. Lee, J. Rousseau,
R. Stampton, M. van der Staay
and K. Doerr, M. Gomes, J. Nakagawa,
K. Rottova, C. Shortle;
O. Aubert, C. Colson, Y. Kyrkos (models)

Consultants
Arup (structure and services);
Lerch, Bates & Associates
(vertical transportation);
Broadway Malyan
(consulting architect)

Phase Two, 2004-2012
Design team
J. Moolhuijzen (partner in charge),
W. Matthews (associate in charge),
B. Akkerhuis, G. Bannatyne,
E. Chen, G. Reid with O. Barthe,
J. Carter, V. Delfaud, M. Durand,
E. Fitzpatrick, S. Joly, G. Longoni,
C. Maxwell-Mahon, J.B. Mothes,
M. Paré, J. Rousseau, I. Tristrant,
A. Vachette, J. Winrow and O. Doule,
J. Leroy, L. Petermann;
O. Aubert, C. Colson, Y. Kyrkos (models)

Consultants
WSP Cantor Seinuk (structure);
Arup (building services);
Lerch, Bates & Associates
(vertical transportation);
Davis Langdon (cost consultant);
Townshend Architects (landscape);
Pascall+Watson
(executive architect for the station)

The Shard

Volume a cura di / Book edited by
Lia Piano

Concezione e realizzazione del volume
Book conception and realization
Lia Piano e Franco Origoni
con / with
Joost Moolhuijzen (partner RPBW)
William Matthews (associate RPBW)
e / and
Renzo Piano Building Workshop:
Elena Spadavecchia

Con la partecipazione di
With the partecipation of
Renzo Piano Building Workshop:
Bart Akkerhuis
Stefania Canta
Chiara Casazza
Eileen Chen
Antonio Porcile
Fondazione Renzo Piano:
Nicoletta Durante
Giovanna Giusto

Progetto grafico e impaginazione
Layout
Franco Origoni e Anna Steiner
con / with
Roberta Cesani

Traduzione / Translation
Miranda Westwood
e / and
Verto Group Srl

Concezione della collana editoriale
Conception of the book series
Lia Piano
Franco Origoni
Giorgio Bianchi
Milly Rossato Piano
Stefania Canta

Prestampa / Prepress
Elleviemme
Stampa / Print
Grafiche Antiga

Tutti i diritti sono riservati. Nessuna parte
di questo libro può essere riprodotta,
riutilizzata o trasferita in alcuna forma
o mezzo (elettronico, elettrostatico,
meccanico, registrazione su nastro,
copia fotostatica, trascrizione o altro)
senza il permesso dell'editore.

All right reserved. No part of this publication
may be reproduced, stored in a retrieval
system or transmitted, in any form
or by any means, electronic, mechanical,
photocopying, recording or otherwise,
without the prior permission
of Fondazione Renzo Piano.

Crediti Fotografici
Photos Credits
Google
Gabriele Basilico
Gianni Berengo Gardin
Hayes Davidson and John Maclean
Michel Denancé
Gregory Fonne
Nic Lehoux
Antony Lycett
Ben Marshall
Lee Maudsley
Hamish McKenzie
Museum of London Archaeology
Lewis Quinn
Sam Roberts
RPBW, Bart Akkerhuis
RPBW, Grant Bannatyne
RPBW, Stefania Canta
RPBW, Jack Carter
RPBW, Donald Hart
RPBW, Shunji Ishida
RPBW, William Matthews
RPBW, Joost Moolhuijzen
RPBW, Maurits van der Staay
RWDI
Renée Smith
Rob Telford
Townshend Landscape Architects
Nikolas Ventourakis
WSP
WSP, Ron Slade
Production Still from 'Common Sky'.
Director Robert McKillop,
photographer Sam Roberts

© Fondazione Renzo Piano
Editore Fondazione Renzo Piano